The Complete
AVOCADO
Cookbook

The Complete AVOCADO Cookbook

CHRISTINE HEASLIP

BAY BOOKS
SYDNEY & LONDON

About the Author

While operating her own restaurant for six years in the North Coast region of New South Wales, Christine Heaslip discovered a multiplicity of ways of using avocados imaginatively in her dishes.

With avocados in abundant supply she was inspired to experiment widely, and soon found her creative dishes were in great demand, both in the restaurant and at her dinner parties.

When one of her dishes, Oriental Stuffed Avocado, won a State competition she set out on the path which led to her compiling this cookbook.

Christine is married and has two children.

Photography by Ashley Barber

Published by Bay Books
61-69 Anzac Parade,
Kensington NSW 2033

Publisher: George Barber

Copyright © Christine Heaslip, 1984

National Library of Australia
Card number and ISBN 0 85835 559 0

The publishers would like to thank the following organisations for their assistance during the photographing of dishes for this book: Fred Pazzoti Pty Ltd and Country Floors (for tiles); David Jones (Australia) Pty Ltd (for glassware, cutlery, chinaware and kitchenware); Slatecraft (for slate).

Tagliatelle avocado
Recipe page 41

CONTENTS

INTRODUCTION

The avocado is a gourmet food that is natural, wholesome, easy to prepare and not too expensive to buy. Above all it is versatile. The variety of the recipes in this book reflects the great adaptability of the avocado which I feel most cooks have not yet even begun to exploit. If you have an avocado on hand you have the basis for any number of quick, wholesome family meals; you also have a splendid ingredient for whipping up a 'dressy' sauce or providing extravagant touches to a special meal. All these recipes are original creations resulting from my own experimenting with avocados. There is a recipe for all tastes and all occasions. You and your guests will be surprised and delighted at some of the spectacular and unusual ways of cooking and presenting this beautiful fruit.

Most people use avocados in fairly simple ways, such as tossed in a salad, sliced on toast or combined with a little lemon juice or vinaigrette and served as an entrée. (One of my favourites is to blend avocado in a milkshake with a little honey to sweeten.) However, a little-known but most rewarding way of using avocados is in desserts. Their smooth, creamy texture lends a particular richness to many sweet dishes. They can simply be diced and included in a fruit salad, blended in a sauce to pour over fruit (bananas are especially good) or puréed with other ingredients to produce a rich flan or cheesecake filling. Unaccountably the avocado is not widely used in sweet dishes: I am still experimenting in this area and constantly coming up with new and unusual flavour combinations. Perhaps the most stunning desserts in this book, both for their taste and appearance, are Green Gateau and Avocado Almondine Meringue. They are great fun to cook and present, as I am sure you will discover.

Of all the main meals my favourite is probably Crusty Stuffed Avocado. It was a great thrill to discover this tempting way of presenting avocados whole. In all recipes I have tried to use fresh, wholesome ingredients: wholemeal flour rather than white; honey or raw sugar rather than refined; fresh fruit, vegetables and herbs; very little salt and, in general, no highly refined or processed products. The recipes, however, can be adjusted, to suit your own tastes. Please consider the following points when altering recipes: if you substitute white flour for wholemeal, use a little extra as wholemeal flour more readily absorbs liquid; if using honey instead of sugar you will need slightly more dry ingredients to achieve the same consistency.

Though justifiably considered a delicacy, avocados are also nutritious and easily digestible which makes them an ideal food for babies and young children. Mashed or puréed, alone or in combination with other ingredients they can be served to babies as one of their very first foods.

A set of metric spoons is an important piece of kitchen equipment and will be most useful in calculating proportions in these recipes. The chapter headings are intended as a guide only; you will find that most of the recipes can be readily adapted to different types of meals. Most of the entrées, for instance, if made in larger quantities will stand very nicely as lunches or main meals. Some desserts, such as the fruit salad, make delightful summer breakfasts. So use your own style and imagination to get the most out of this book!

I hope you will find, as I did, that these recipes are as enjoyable to prepare as they are delicious to eat.

Ricotta avocado flan
Recipe page 52

Facts about the avocado

The avocado is native to Mexico and Central America. Indeed its name comes from the ancient Aztec name for the fruit, *ahuacatl*. By the time Columbus discovered America the avocado had spread to the north of the continent and south as far as Peru. It was later introduced to the West Indies in the early 16th century.

The trees are mostly evergreen and can grow to a height of around 12 metres. There are over 70 recognised varieties of avocado in Australia alone and the fruit is exceedingly variable in shape, size and colour. The three main commercial varieties are Fuerte, Sharwil and Hass; these come into maturity at different times giving a spread of production from around April to December. The Sharwil variety is pear-shaped with a smooth, green skin and is harvested from May to June. Hass is a smaller variety with a rough, pebbled skin which turns purplish-black on maturity; it is in season from August to December. The hybrid Fuerte is picked from April to May; it has a slightly pebbled green skin. Another — the kuke — is a relatively new type, commonly known as the cocktail avocado. This is not a separate variety, but an immature avocado. It is small and bullet-shaped and, because it has virtually no seed, is well suited to being sliced and presented in a variety of ways.

Avocados are usually sold green. They will take several days to ripen if left in a warm, dark place; longer if kept refrigerated. Beware of overripe fruit, it develops an unpleasant, musty taste and is not useable.

Nutritionally, the avocado has a lower carbohydrate content that other fruits, containing less than 1 per cent sugar. As much as 30 per cent of the weight of the fruit is oil, but bear in mind that most of this is in the form of unsaturated fats. These do not increase cholesterol levels in the bloodstream and therefore offer safe and healthful eating. Avocados contain significant amounts of vitamins A, B, B2, C and E, and vital minerals including potassium, phosphorus, magnesium, iron and several trace elements. They are also rich in protein. It is important to note that this is a complete protein containing all nine of the essential amino acids required for the manufacture of new tissue in the body.

Weight-conscious people may be surprised to learn that one half of an avocado (an average serving) contains only 552 kilojoules (or 138 calories).

Avocado cutting techniques

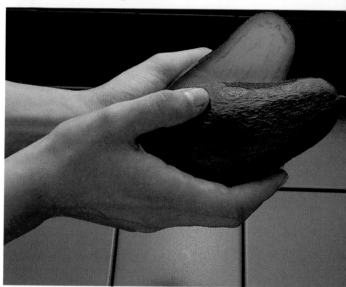

1: *Cut avocado lengthwise*

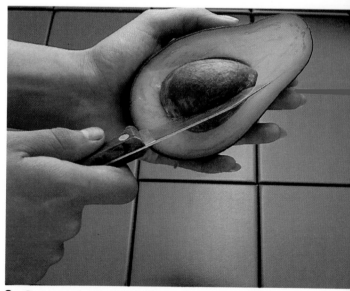

2: *Twist the halves apart*

3: *Cut into the seed and lift*

Useful Hints

1. Avocados will discolour easily once cut, but you can deal with this problem by:
   coating with lemon juice using a pastry brush;
   covering with very thin slices of lemon; and
   leaving the seed in one half of the avocado which will slow down discoloration a little.
2. Avocado pieces can be frozen fairly successfully if tossed with a good amount of lemon juice and put into freezer bags. Once thawed, the avocado can be used for purées, sauces, dips or any dish where appearance is not important.
3. Avocados are ripe when the flesh is soft but holds its shape well. Overripe avocados are pretty well impossible to use.
4. When cooking with avocado, it is important not to boil whatever it is in or to overcook it, as the unique and subtle flavour of the avocado is easily destroyed. They can develop a bitter flavour if cooked improperly.
5. Uncooked dessert dishes will usually keep well in the refrigerator for two days. Cooked dishes will be edible cold the next day, but reheating will often destroy the flavour.

Preparation

How to cut and prepare avocados:

Cut avocado lengthwise into halves.

Twist to separate.

Insert a sharp knife into the seed, twist and lift seed out.

To make avocado balls use a melon baller or round metal ½ teaspoon measure.

To peel avocado, strip skin from fruit beginning at narrow end.

Cavity side down, cut lengthwise or, for crescents, crosswise; to dice or cube cut both ways.

To make rings, cut around avocado crosswise with tip of knife to form rings, then remove skin.

Warning

Care has to be taken when buying avocados that are out of season or imported. If an avocado is picked too early — so that its oil content is at a level insufficient to allow for the full development of its flavour during ripening — or if it is picked too late in the season — when it is stale — its flavour will be affected. In some cases imported avocados that may have been placed in cold storage before being presented for sale have been known to overripen. This can result in an avocado that quickly browns when cut open, making for an unattractive appearance and an unsavoury taste.

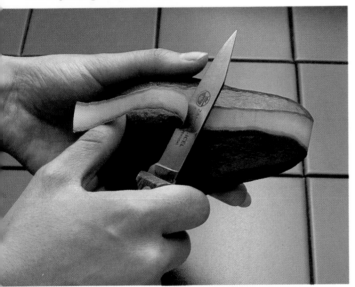

4: *Preparing avocado balls*

5: *When peeling, begin at the narrow end*

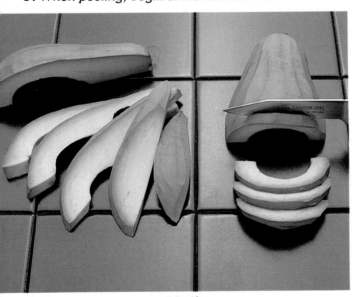

6: *Cutting crescents and half rings*

Some Special Ingredients

Agar-Agar

Sea vegetable gelatine. High in calcium and other minerals.

Capers

The unopened flower buds of the caper bush, commonly grown in the Mediterranean.

Coriander

A herb similar to parsley when fresh, but widely used in Indian cooking as a spice in powder form.

Cumin

An aromatic Indian spice.

Julienne Strips

Vegetables sliced into approximate 2cm x 2cm strips that require very little cooking.

Pepitas

Edible green pumpkin seeds.

Pine Nuts

Kernels from the cone of the Mediterranean Umbrella pine tree.

Pita Bread

Flat bread which is used widely in Mediterranean and Middle Eastern countries.

Sorrel

A herb widely used with fish because of its distinct lemon flavour; similar in appearance to English spinach.

Tagliatelle

Long, thin, ribbon-like noodles, available in white, wholemeal or spinach flavour.

Tahini

A paste made from sesame seeds, much like peanut butter but very smooth.

Tamari

Similar to soy sauce but tamari is aged longer and has a slightly different flavour.

ENTRÉES

This section contains a wide variety of recipes, enabling you to use avocados as individually and imaginatively as you wish. The traditional avocado half is presented with some interesting variations, including the prize-winning Oriental Stuffed Avocado — a simple but exotic recipe which captures the flavours of the Orient.

Some of these entrées make delightful lunches if served in larger quantities. For instance, the Gardinera Avocado Mini-Pizza and the Crumble-topped Avocado Quiche make a satisfying, complete meal with the addition of fresh vegetables or a light salad.

There is a basic avocado soup recipe as well as one for Sorrel and Avocado Soup. Variations to the basic soup recipe are not included, but almost anything can be added to suit individual tastes, such as zucchini (chopped or puréed), prawns (and other seafood), cheese or herbs.

...ffed potato
...pe page 22

Avocado Soup

A superb soup served hot or cold

2 avocados
2 cups chicken or strong
    vegetable stock
juice 1/2 lemon
1/4 cup cream
fresh ground pepper
salt to taste

Purée avocado with stock and lemon juice in blender. Heat gently until hot. Don't boil.

Season and add cream before serving. If serving cold, there is no need to cook the soup, just purée as above and add seasonings and cream.

Note: This soup can be served with croutons or a crusty breadstick and sprinkled with chopped watercress.

Serves 4

Sorrel and Avocado Soup

The superb lemon flavour of fresh sorrel blends beautifully with avocado. English spinach can be substituted if sorrel is unobtainable.

500g fresh sorrel leaves
50g butter
600mL vegetable stock
150mL cream
2 avocados
fresh ground pepper
dash lemon juice, if
    spinach is used

Mash avocados and mix with a little of the cream.

Shred sorrel leaves and gently cook in butter for 5 minutes. Cool. Put stock in blender with cooked sorrel and purée until smooth.

Return to saucepan and heat again over moderate heat, adding cream and pepper at the very end with the mashed avocado. Serve hot.

Serves 4

Sorrel and avocado soup

Prawn and Avocado Pâté

250g small prawns,
  shelled
2 avocados
60g butter
3 tablespoons plain flour
1 cup milk
½ cup sour cream
½ teaspoon Dijon
  mustard

freshly ground pepper
2 teaspoons gelatine
¼ cup water
¼ cup mayonnaise
1 tablespoon lemon juice
chopped parsley and half
  avocado to garnish

Step 1: *Melt butter and add sifted flour over heat*

Melt butter and add flour. Remove from heat and gradually stir in milk and sour cream. Stir until well combined and sauce thickens. Simmer for 5 minutes over low heat. Cool slightly.

Blend sauce and avocado in a blender until smooth. Chop prawns finely, reserving 12 for garnish. Mix through avocado sauce. Add mustard and freshly ground pepper.

Sprinkle gelatine over water and dissolve over hot water. Add gelatine to avocado mixture. Cool to lukewarm. Mix through mayonnaise and lemon juice.

Spoon into 6 individual dishes or pâté bowls and refrigerate for a few hours. Garnish with chopped parsley, 2 prawns each person and a little finely sliced avocado.

Serve with Melba toast or crudités.

Note: a slight discoloration can occur if avocados are not freshly ripened. Serves 6

Avocado Pâté

2 large avocados
4 hard-boiled eggs, finely
  chopped
2 tablespoons lemon
  juice
2 cloves garlic, crushed
2 teaspoons chopped
  parsley

1 tablespoon chopped
  fresh mint
freshly ground pepper
salt to taste
¼ cup sour cream or
  mayonnaise
⅛ teaspoon sweet
  paprika

Cut avocados in half, remove seed and carefully scoop out flesh and put in a bowl. Save the avocado skins for serving.

Mash avocado with all remaining ingredients. Replace mixture into shells, smoothing down so as to keep avocado shape.

Garnish with lemon twist and a sprig of parsley and serve with Melba toast or crackers.

Note: Slight discoloration can occur if avocados are not freshly ripened.

Serves 4

Step 2: *Blend sauce and avocado in blender till smooth*

Step 3: *Mix chopped prawns through the avocado sauce*

Prawn and avocado pâte

Fried Avocado

Frying is probably the simplest way of cooking avocado. A lemon sauce or Hollandaise sauce will make it dressier.

avocados, sliced cross-
    ways
beaten egg
breadcrumbs (can be
    combined with sesame
    seeds, caraway seeds
    or a pinch or two of
    your favourite herb)
butter for frying

Dip avocado slices into egg, then breadcrumbs and fry gently until golden brown on both sides. Handle carefully so as not to break up the avocado.

Garnish with fresh dill or tarragon and a slice of lemon.

Jade Balls

Flavours reminiscent of the Orient combine beautifully with the versatile avocado.

500g ricotta cheese
2 avocados, mashed
1 medium onion, finely
    chopped
1/2 cup dry breadcrumbs
1 beaten egg
breadcrumbs for coating
oil for frying

Mash ricotta with avocados and mix in onion and breadcrumbs. Form into balls the size of a golf ball and dip in beaten egg, then breadcrumbs.

Cook until golden brown in a little oil, on all sides. Drain well on absorbent paper and serve with dipping sauce in little Chinese dishes. Garnish with shreds of shallots.

Dipping Sauce

1 teaspoon sherry
2 tablespoons honey
1 clove garlic, crushed

1 teaspoon grated fresh
    ginger
1/8 cup tamari or soy
    sauce

Combine all ingredients in a small jar and allow to marinate for a few hours before use.

Serves 6

Crumble-topped Avocado Quiche

In the past few years quiches have become very popular. They provide an excellent vehicle for featuring the delicate flavour of the avocado.

Pastry

250g plain flour
200g soft butter

Filling

2 avocados
125g cream cheese
4 eggs
4 finely chopped shallots
1 cup cream, or 1/2 milk
    and 1/2 cream
pinch nutmeg
freshly ground pepper
salt to taste

Fried avocado

Cut butter into flour with a long-bladed knife, then rub in with fingertips until it resembles breadcrumbs. Form into a ball, wrap in plastic wrap and chill for at least 1 hour before using.

Grease a pie dish or quiche tray and press pastry into dish with fingertips evenly. (This pastry has so much butter it is too crumbly to roll out, but you can use your favourite shortcrust pastry instead.) Prick all over with a fork and bake for 10 minutes at 200°C (400°F).

Blend avocado, cream cheese, eggs, cream, nutmeg and seasonings in blender until smooth. Mix in shallots and pour into pie crust.

Bake at 180°C (350°F) for 30 to 40 minutes or until set.

Crumble

2 tablespoons sesame
  seeds

½ cup breadcrumbs
60g melted butter

Toss melted butter with seeds and breadcrumbs and spread evenly over top of quiche when quiche is just starting to set (about 15 to 20 minutes) before end of cooking time. Crumble should be browned before removing quiche.

Note: Quiche can be allowed to cool down for about 15 minutes before serving as it is just as nice at room temperature. It will keep well for the next day too.

Serves 8-10

Gardinera Avocado Mini-Pizza

Fresh garden vegetables, avocado and cheese baked on pita bread all add up to a dish that's a great success with children. These little pizzas also make a good lunch.

2 mini-sized pieces of pita bread
1 avocado, thinly sliced
1 tomato, thinly sliced
1 zucchini, thinly sliced
1 onion, finely chopped
1 tablespoon finely chopped capsicum
1 tablespoon chopped parsley
2 tablespoons tomato paste
1 cup grated cheese, or ½ cup fresh Parmesan and ½ cup Cheddar cheese
optional: a few chopped olives as garnish

Mix all ingredients except cheese in a bowl. Spread evenly over pita bread, making sure it is covered right up to the edge. Top with sliced avocado and then grated cheese.

Put in preheated oven at 220°C (425°F), until cheese has melted and is bubbling and brown, or put under grill (not too close) until done.

Serves 2

Gardinera avocado mini-pizza

Avocado Gnocchi

A very versatile dish which you can serve as an entrée, main meal or accompaniment.

250g ricotta cheese
150g fresh Parmesan
  cheese, grated
1 egg
¼ teaspoon nutmeg
2 avocados, mashed
50g butter
plain flour

Mash avocados with the ricotta cheese, half the Parmesan cheese and the egg and nutmeg. Mix well.

Form the mixture into balls the size of small eggs, using a spoon and the palm of your hand to mould them. Roll eggs lightly in the flour.

Bring a large pot of salted water to the boil and drop the gnocchi in, 4 or 5 at a time. Simmer gently until the gnocchi rise to the surface (about 2 minutes).

Remove from the pot with a slotted spoon and arrange in a well greased, flat oven dish. Melt butter and pour over the gnocchi; sprinkle with remaining Parmesan cheese.

Place under hot grill for a few minutes until cheese turns golden brown.

Variation: Serve with this piquant tomato-herb sauce.

Tomato–Herb Sauce

500g tomatoes, chopped
1 bay leaf
1 small onion, chopped
1 tablespoon chopped
  parsley
¼ teaspoon dried basil
1 clove garlic, crushed
1 teaspoon sweet paprika
¼ cup red wine

Cook all ingredients together for about 1 hour or until sauce is thick. Stir occasionally.

Mixture can be puréed in a blender if a smooth sauce is preferred, but allow to cool a little first.

Note: For variation, ½ cup sour cream can be stirred in or ¼ cup ordinary cream. A dessertspoon of tomato paste can be added for a richer tomato flavour.

Serves 4-6

Avocado al pesto

Opposite:
Asparagus-avocado mushrooms

Avocado al Pesto

A classic Italian dressing served with a classic food.

1 1/2 cups olive oil
8 cloves garlic, peeled
2 cups fresh basil leaves
   (increase for a thicker
   sauce)
2/3 cup freshly grated
   Parmesan cheese
2 large avocados, sliced
shredded lettuce or curly
   endive

Blend oil, garlic and basil in a blender until smooth and thick. Mix in grated cheese. Heat sauce in double boiler until hot, stirring constantly.

To serve, arrange sliced avocado on a bed of shredded lettuce or endive. Spoon hot sauce over avocado. A little cream may be added to sauce when heating.

Note: This sauce freezes well without the addition of the cream.

Serves 4

Asparagus–Avocado Mushrooms

The delicate flavours of avocado and asparagus are encased in open field-mushroom caps.

8 large mushrooms,
   stalks gently twisted
   out
1 avocado
4 fresh or tinned
   asparagus spears
juice of 1 lemon
optional: dash or two of
   Tabasco sauce
grated cheese
sour cream to garnish

Arrange half the asparagus spears over mushrooms. Finely chop the remaining asparagus. Mash these with avocado, lemon juice, tabasco and a little freshly ground black pepper.

Pile into mushrooms, allowing mixture to sit slightly above level of the mushroom. Sprinkle over grated cheese and grill until bubbly.

Note: Can be served raw. Garnish with a little sour cream and paprika. Serves 4

Avocado-stuffed potato

Mushroom-stuffed Avocado

This dish is a delight for those who love the combination of garlic and mushrooms.

1 large avocado, halved
350g mushrooms, sliced
50g butter
2 cloves garlic, crushed

Sauté mushrooms and garlic in butter until mushrooms are just tender but not mushy. Spoon into centre of avocado halves and top with cocktail sauce.

Cocktail Sauce

½ cup cream　　　　　　*½ teaspoon tarragon*
1 teaspoon tomato paste　*4 drops Tabasco sauce*
2 teaspoons lemon juice　*½ teaspoon sweet*
1 teaspoon tamari or soy　*paprika*
sauce　　　　　　　　*freshly ground pepper*

Heat ingredients in saucepan until fairly hot. Do not boil. Cool slightly before serving. If a thicker sauce is desired, it can be thickened with a little arrowroot or cornflour.
　Garnish with slices of fresh mushroom and lemon.

Serves 2

Avocado-stuffed Potato

This makes a first course with a difference, and is a wonderful addition to most foods with which you would serve baked potatoes.

2 medium sweet potatoes
*   or ordinary potatoes*
1 avocado
2 teaspoons butter
1 medium onion, very
*   finely chopped*
freshly ground pepper
salt to taste

Bake whole, unpeeled potatoes in 220°C (425°F) oven until soft, but firm enough to stuff. Cool.
　Cut evenly in half and scoop out flesh, allowing a small rim inside potato for shape. Blend or mash avocado with potato flesh and mix with butter, onion and seasonings. Replace in potato shell and top with a little knob of butter, if desired. Bake at 200°C (400°F) until heated through and lightly browned on top. Dust with paprika.
　Note: Grated cheese or breadcrumbs can be cooked on top when reheating. A dollop of sour cream completes the dish. Serves 4

Avocado–Chicken Waldorf

This combination of avocado, chicken, apple, celery, walnuts and mayonnaise can be served as a first course or as a salad.

200g chopped chicken,
*   cooked*
2 avocados, chopped
1 small red apple, finely
*   chopped*
1 stick celery, chopped
1 tablespoon lemon juice
½ cup mayonnaise
½ cup walnuts

Combine all ingredients. Serve on a lettuce leaf and garnish with one or two whole walnuts and avocado slices.

Serves 4

Mushroom-stuffed avocado

Avodamia Nest

You can use your own imagination for fillings and toppings for this basic idea.

Nest

2 avocados
2 beaten eggs
ground raw macadamia
    nuts to coat
oil for frying

Fillings

8 large mushrooms,
    finely sliced
1 medium onion, finely
    sliced
sour cream to garnish
or
1½ cups grated cheese
4 slices ham, finely
    chopped
2 sticks celery, finely
    chopped
or
2 tomatoes, diced, or
    cherry tomatoes
4 shallots, finely chopped
½ teaspoon dried basil
1 clove garlic, crushed
125 g cream cheese,
    finely diced

Cut avocados in half, remove seeds and carefully peel away skin.

Dip avocado into beaten egg, then into ground macadamia nuts. Rather than move the avocado half around too much, it is easier to toss the nuts over it with a spoon.

Fry in shallow oil on both sides until golden brown.

Sauté onions and mushrooms in a little butter until soft but not mushy.

Place in 'avodamia' nest and garnish with a swirl of sour cream and a sprinkling of paprika.

Toss cheese, ham and celery together and pile into avodamia nest. Grill under moderate heat until cheese is bubbling and browning slightly.

Mix all ingredients together and pile into avodamia nest. Bake in a very hot oven until filling is heated through.

Note: If the last filling is used, don't brown the avodamia nest quite as much to allow for browning in the oven.

Serves 4

Salmon and Avocado Hollandaise

A combination of very thin slices of smoked salmon served on avocado and topped with Hollandaise sauce.

*3 avocados, halved,
    seeded and thinly
    sliced
200g smoked salmon,
    cut into thin strips
6 lettuce leaves
6 lemon twists and
    parsley to garnish*

Twist thin strips of salmon and serve on lettuce leaves if desired. Spoon over sauce and garnish with a lemon slice, fresh dill and avocado.

Hollandaise Sauce

*180g butter
3 egg yolks
1 tablespoon lemon juice
freshly ground pepper
pinch salt*

Melt the butter. Put eggs, seasonings and lemon juice in a blender and combine. Allow melted butter to cool for 1 minute.

While the blender is in motion, very gradually drip the melted butter through the hole in the lid until sauce is smooth. Serve immediately.

Note: This sauce can be temperamental if you're not used to dealing with emulsifying sauces. Just take it slowly, step by step.

Serves 6

Lemange Avocado

A refreshing change from the simple avocado vinaigrette.

3 avocado halves with
  seeds removed

Dressing

4 tablespoons olive oil
4 tablespoons orange
  juice
3 tablespoons lemon
  juice
1 tablespoon honey
pinch salt
freshly ground pepper

Shake all ingredients in a jar. Allow to stand for at least 30 minutes before using or, ideally, chill dressing before serving.

To serve, arrange avocado half on a lettuce or chicory leaf or in an avocado dish. Spoon over dressing and garnish with an orange slice and finely chopped parsley.

Serves 3

Opposite: Filo avocado-chicken
Recipe page 34

28

MAIN MEALS

Crêpes, pastries, roulades and many other interesting dishes are featured in this section. Some can be prepared in very little time; others need more of your attention. But always bear in mind the delicate flavour of the avocado and never reheat or overcook a meal, as it would be spoiled completely.

Crêpes can be prepared ahead of time, and the avocado filling added just before serving. Remember that crêpes are always more tasty when heated with the filling inside, rather than before the filling is added.

The Crusty Stuffed Avocado presents the avocado whole. It is a very substantial meal and lends itself to the inclusion of a filling to suit your own taste, be it seafood, poultry or vegetables.

Beef Avocado Moutarde

1 large avocado, sliced
½ bunch spinach,
  chopped
60g butter
handful finely chopped
  fresh mint
250g thinly sliced beef
2 tablespoons butter

Sauté spinach in melted butter with mint until soft. Keep warm in shallow baking dish.

Sauté beef slices in butter on both sides until browned and cooked according to taste.

Sauce

2 hard-boiled egg yolks
1 teaspoon French
  mustard
1 raw egg yolk
150 mL thickened cream

Mash hard-boiled egg yolks with mustard and raw egg yolk. Heat in double boiler gently with cream until hot. Be careful not to overcook.

To assemble, place cooked beef slices on bed of spinach. Place sliced avocado on top of beef and spoon over the mustard sauce. Keep warm in the oven or serve immediately.

Garnish with slices of fresh avocado and finely chopped fresh herbs.

Serves 2

Avocado Schnitzel

The delicate flavour of veal subtly combined with avocado makes this well-known recipe even more enjoyable.

4 thin veal escalopes
juice of 1 lemon
1-2 eggs
1 cup dry breadcrumbs
4 tablespoons butter
4 thick slices Emmenthal
  cheese
2 avocados, sliced

Brush veal with lemon juice on both sides. Toss veal in beaten egg and then crumbs. Heat butter and cook veal on both sides for about 3 minutes or until golden brown.

Place sliced avocado on each veal scallop, top with cheese slices and grill until melted and heated through; alternatively, place lid on frypan and heat gently until cheese melts and avocado is heated.

Garnish with lemon slices and a green leafy herb or finely diced red pepper.

Serves 4

Baked Snapper with Avocado

This dish, apart from looking impressive with the whole snappers has a delicately flavoured avocado stuffing. It also can be topped with the Avocado Fish Sauce. (See recipe on p. 69.)

2 whole snapper,
   approx. ½ kg each
1 tablespoon melted
   butter
2 tablespoons lemon
   juice
2 slices bread, crumbled
1 onion, thinly sliced
1 stick celery, finely sliced
½ teaspoon dried thyme
fresh ground pepper
salt to taste
1 egg, beaten lightly
2 avocados, finely
   chopped

Brush cavity of fish with melted butter. Mix crumbled bread, lemon juice, onion, celery, thyme, pepper, salt, egg and avocados together. Stuff cavity of fish with avocado stuffing and secure with skewers.

Bake at 200°C on a greased tray for 30-40 minutes or until fish flakes easily with a fork. Remove skewers before serving. Garnish with finely chopped chives.

Serves 2

Avocado Veal Birds in Port Wine

750g thin veal steaks
4 tablespoons butter
2 tablespoons plain flour
freshly ground pepper
salt to taste
2 onions, finely chopped
½ cup stock
¼ cup port wine
½ cup cream
2 tablespoons flour

Spread a heaped tablespoon of avocado stuffing onto each piece of steak. Roll up and secure with a skewer or string. Coat rolls with seasoned flour.

Melt butter in a frypan and brown rolls on all sides. Remove to serving dish and keep warm.

Cook onion in remaining juices in frypan. Mix in flour and add stock and wine. Stir while cooking for about 15 minutes, then mix in cream.

Spoon sauce over rolls and serve. Some may prefer to place rolls in the oven for 10 minutes to allow all the flavours to mingle.

Stuffing

¼ cup finely chopped
   shallots
1 tablespoon finely
   chopped parsley
1 tablespoon fresh thyme
   leaves
grated rind of 1 lemon
2 avocados, mashed
1 cup soft breadcrumbs

Mix shallots, parsley, thyme, lemon rind and mashed avocado together. Work in breadcrumbs.

Serves 6

Avocado veal birds
in port wine

Step 1: *Cook fillets, dusted with flour, in butter and oil*

Step 2: *Place fillets on pastry, spread with mustard, top with avocado*

Filo Avocado–Chicken

Although it has been used in Middle Eastern countries for many years, filo pastry is only now becoming a common household item. It can be used with any filling, and this one is especially easy and tasty.

200 g filo pastry sheets
2 teaspoons dried tarragon
2 teaspoons French mustard
6 chicken fillets or 3 whole chicken breasts with bones removed
3 avocados, thinly sliced
plain flour

freshly ground pepper and salt to taste
2 tablespoons oil
melted butter for brushing pastry

Mix tarragon, mustard and seasonings together. Dust chicken fillet with flour and cook in butter and oil until nicely browned on both sides. Cool.

Using 2 sheets of filo pastry for each person, brush one sheet with melted butter, cover with second sheet and brush again. Fold in half and brush again.

Place one fillet in centre at the end of the pastry, spread over a little tarragon mustard, then top with avocado slices. Fold slices of pastry over the chicken to completely enclose. Repeat with remaining chicken.

Place on greased oven tray, brush pastry tops with butter and bake at 200°C (400°F) for 10 minutes, reducing heat to 180°C (350°F) for a further 10 to 15 minutes. Filo rolls should be a light golden brown. Serve with seasonal vegetables.

Note: you can prepare this dish up to two hours before serving time if it is kept in the refrigerator; heat for 10 minutes before serving.

Serves 6

Step 3: *Fold over pastry*

Filo avocado chicken

Chicken and Avocado Pie Béchamel

Pastry

2 cups plain flour
125g softened butter
½ cup cream

Cut butter into flour with knife and then rub in with fingertips until mixture resembles breadcrumbs. Mix cream in with a spoon, adding a little more if your flour absorbs more liquid.

Form dough into ball and refrigerate (in summer) for 1 hour before using; in winter, covered at room temperature for 1 hour.

Grease round pie dish and line with half of pastry. Add filling and top with remainder of pastry.

Filling

1 x 2kg chicken *8 peppercorns*
6 cups water *4 cloves garlic*
2 leeks or onions *1 teaspoon salt*
2 bay leaves *3 avocados, chopped*
3 sprigs parsley

Place whole chicken and rest of ingredients in large saucepan. Bring to the boil, cover and simmer over low heat for about 1¼ hours or until chicken is tender. Remove chicken from liquid and cool. Reserve stock.

Chop chicken into long pieces and toss with Béchamel sauce and chopped avocado.

Béchamel Sauce

60g butter *½ cup chopped parsley*
50g plain flour *salt and pepper*
300mL cream
450mL reserved stock
1 teaspoon tarragon

Melt butter in heavy saucepan. Add flour and stir well. Remove from heat and gradually stir in stock and tarragon. Return to heat and cook, stirring, till mixture thickens.

Add cream and stir again till mixture is a very thick sauce. Add salt, pepper and parsley.

Glaze top of pie with a beaten egg or a little milk and bake at 200°C (400°F) for 20 to 30 minutes or until golden brown on top.

Serves 6-8

Seafood Avocado Mille-Feuille

An easy-to-prepare dish that is very impressive at a dinner party. The complementary flavours seem to be made for each other.

500g puff pastry
2 cups béchamel sauce
2 avocados, chopped
    and tossed with juice of
    1 lemon
2 medium sized fish
    fillets, sea perch is very
    suitable
4 king prawns
fresh dill sprig to garnish

Roll out pastry and cut into 4 equal squares or rectangles. Bake in 200°C (400°F) oven for 20 minutes or until golden brown. Cut a little slit in top and cool on wire rack.

Fry fish fillets in a little butter until cooked. Break neatly into pieces.

Mix cooked fish, cooked prawns and chopped lemon avocado into béchamel sauce and very gently heat until filling is well warmed.

This filling is best heated in a frying pan, so that it does not have to be stirred quite as much.

To serve, cut cooked pastry squares in half. The inside pastry can be scooped out to give a neater effect, but many prefer it whole.

Spoon in the seafood-avocado filling and replace the lid if desired. Decorate with a little filling around the edge of the puff pastry case and then garnish with the dill sprig.

Note: Nothing more than a light salad needs to be served with this dish.

Serves 4

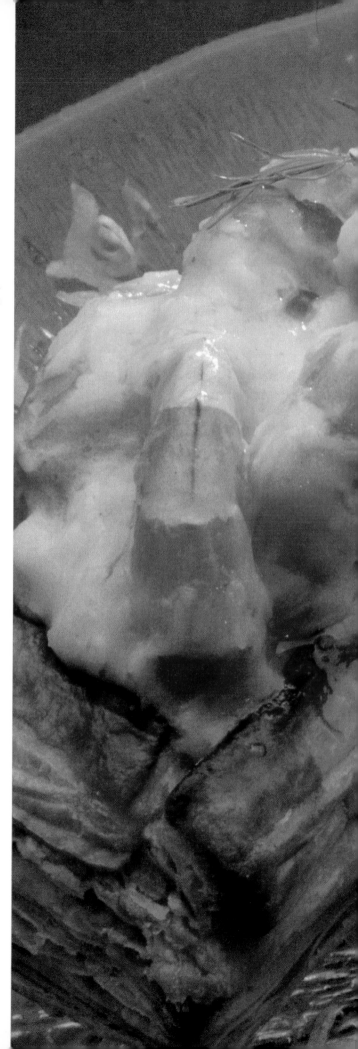

Spinach–Avocado Parcels

8 large spinach leaves,
   stems carefully
   removed
2 avocados, diced
250g cottage cheese
2 tablespoons chopped
   parsley
2 tablespoons chopped
   fresh mint
1 large onion, sautéed in
   a little butter with ½
   teaspoon sweet
   paprika
1 cup cooked brown rice

Mix cottage cheese, mint, parsley, sautéed onion and rice. Add avocado. Place equal amounts of filling in centre of each spinach leaf and roll up securely, ensuring edges are folded in.

(Spinach may be put into really hot water for a few minutes to soften it slightly. Drain well before use.)

Steam spinach parcels in a vegetable steamer or Chinese bamboo steamer for a few minutes to allow filling to heat through and spinach to soften.

Serve with a little butter rubbed over the top, with your favourite cheese sauce or fresh Tomato-Herb Sauce.

Serves 4

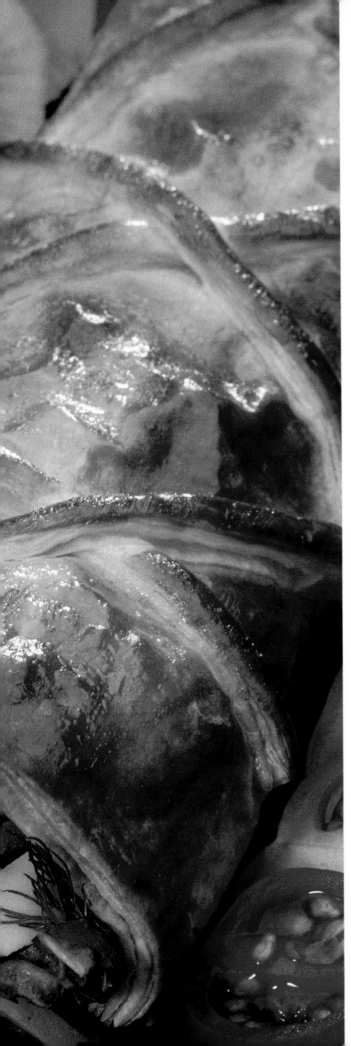

Summer Roll

1 bunch spinach,
  shredded
3 medium carrots, grated
1 large onion, sliced
  thinly
60g butter
3 small sprigs fresh dill or
  ½ teaspoon dried dill
2 avocados, chopped
1 cup mung beans or
  Chinese bean sprouts

Melt butter and sauté onion and carrot for 10 minutes with lid on pan, stirring occasionally. Add spinach and dill.

Stir well and cook further for a few minutes until spinach is soft. Cool.

Add avocados and mix well. Add sprouts.

This filling can be rolled with puff pastry, wholemeal pastry, filo pastry or spring roll sheets.

Place filled rolls on greased tray and cook at 220°C (425°F) until lightly browned.

Glaze pastry with milk and glaze spring roll sheets with melted butter before baking.

Spring Roll

1 cup water
1 cup plain flour
1 egg
1 tablespoon oil

Blend ingredients in blender until smooth, adding more water if too thick. This batter should be of a similar consistency to crêpe batter, allowing for it to thicken as it stands. Leave in refrigerator for 30 minutes.

Heat frypan; when hot turn down to a low heat. Pour batter over pan, tilting so as to move it evenly and thinly over surface.

Cook until batter comes away easily; cook other side 1 minute. These should not be browned at all, like crêpes.

Note: The unfilled spring rolls freeze well, separated with plastic and cooled completely beforehand. They can also be deep-fried in oil, if preferred to baking.

Serves 6

Summer roll

Mexican Fish Balls with Avocado Sauce

500 g fish fillets
4 tablespoons butter
4 shallots, finely chopped
2 slices day-old bread,
   with crusts removed
½ cup milk
1 egg, beaten
1 cup fine dry
   breadcrumbs
1½ tablespoons tomato
   purée
salt and pepper
4 tablespoons oil

Sauté fish fillets in butter for 5 minutes, adding shallots and then cooking for a further 5 minutes. Remove from pan and flake fish finely with fork.

Soak bread in milk for 5 minutes. Squeeze out excess milk, and crumble bread into bowl with fish. Add salt, pepper, egg and tomato purée.

Combine thoroughly, shape into walnut-sized balls and coat with breadcrumbs.

Heat oil in frying pan and cook fish balls on all sides till golden brown. Remove with slotted spoon and drain on paper towels or brown paper. Keep hot.

Sauce

1 cup white wine
juice of ½ lemon
2 tablespoons butter
2 tablespoons flour
½ cup cream
2 avocados, mashed or
   puréed
2 tablespoons fresh (or 1
   teaspoon dried)
   marjoram
salt and pepper

Melt butter in saucepan. Add flour and cook, stirring, for 1 minute. Add white wine gradually. Stir until sauce is thickened and then add marjoram, cream, puréed avocado and lemon juice.

Cook, stirring, for a further 5 to 10 minutes and then pour over cooked fish balls.

Garnish with chillies and fresh lemon.

Serves 4

*Mexican fish balls
with avocado sauce*

Tagliatelle avocado

Tagliatelle Avocado

The pasta, with its varying colours, looks delightful accompanying the avocado, and makes for an easy, satisfying meal served with salad.

450 g wholemeal
   tagliatelle noodles (half
   wholemeal and half
   spinach)
4 avocados, diced
8 cloves garlic, crushed
1 cup fresh basil,
   chopped or 3
   teaspoons dried basil
80 g butter
½ cup chopped parsley
freshly ground pepper
salt to taste
optional: grated
   Parmesan cheese

Cook noodles as directed. Drain and set aside. Melt butter in large saucepan, adding garlic and basil. Sauté 5 minutes.

Add cooked noodles, avocado, parsley and seasonings and toss gently until all ingredients are heated through.

To serve, sprinkle on cheese if desired.

Serves 4

Crusty Stuffed Avocado

Crust

dry breadcrumbs and
  sesame seeds in equal
  proportions
1 teaspoon caraway
  seeds
2 eggs, beaten well
plain flour

Combine breadcrumbs, sesame seeds and caraway seeds. Have ready in deep, wide bowl to coat avocado and do the same for the flour and beaten eggs.

Filling

2 medium avocados
juice of 1 lemon
¾ whole Camembert
  cheese, chopped small
1 clove garlic, crushed
freshly ground pepper
3 tablespoons finely
  chopped fresh herbs
dash or two Tabasco
  sauce

Cut avocados in half lengthways. Scoop out seed and a little of flesh. Mash flesh with cheese, garlic, herbs, tabasco and pepper.

Pour a little lemon juice into avocado shells and put mashed filling back in. Put avocado together again and carefully peel skin away.

Coat whole avocado in flour, then beaten egg, then crumb mixture. Repeat coating process once again.

Fry in hot oil until golden brown (to seal), then bake at about 200°C (400°F) in oven dish until heated through (about 15 minutes). Top with Almond Butter Sauce.

Sauce

2 tablespoons slivered,
  roasted almonds
1 teaspoon sweet paprika
3 tablespoons butter
juice of ¼ lemon

Melt butter and add paprika. Cook for a few minutes then add nuts and lemon juice.

Note: After frying avocado in oil, it may be refrigerated for a while before baking, and then heated in the oven.   Serves 2

Guanajuato Avocado Omelette

1 large avocado,
  chopped
2 tablespoons sour cream
1 tablespoon lemon juice
½ cup grated Mozzarella
  cheese
4 large eggs, beaten well
3 tablespoons butter
fresh ground pepper
salt to taste

Toss avocado, sour cream, lemon juice and cheese in a bowl. Set aside.

Melt butter in a frying pan and evenly coat the pan with it. When butter is foaming, let it subside. Whip pepper and salt through beaten eggs. Pour in beaten eggs and tilt pan so they spread evenly. When omelette starts to set, loosen edges and carefully lift them, tilting pan so the uncooked eggs run to the bottom.

Spoon avocado filling onto one half of the omelette and fold over the other half. Cook over a low heat for about 3 minutes on each side. Serve topped with the chilli sauce if desired (see recipe below).

Chilli Sauce

1 large tomato, finely
  chopped
1 tablespoon tomato
  paste
1 tablespoon fresh
  chillies, very finely
  chopped
2 tablespoons grated
  onion
1 tablespoon cider
  vinegar
1 clove garlic, crushed

Mix all ingredients together and cook for approximately 30 minutes, until thick.

Serves 2

Crusty stuffed avocado

Step 1: *Mash prepared avocado with cheese, garlic, herbs, Tabasco and pepper*

Step 2: *Pile filling into avocado*

Step 3: *Coat avocado with beaten egg and flour*

Walnut and Avocado Roulade

3 tablespoons butter
1/3 cup plain flour
1 cup milk
1 teaspoon French
    mustard
4 eggs, separated
2/3 cup grated cheese

Filling

3 avocados, chopped
2/3 cup walnut pieces
1/2 cup chopped parsley
6 shallots, chopped
1/2 cup freshly grated
    Parmesan cheese

Melt butter and stir in flour until smooth. Cook 1 minute and remove from heat. Gradually add milk and cook over moderate heat, stirring, until thick.

Remove and add mustard and cheese. 250g cooked spinach (with all moisture squeezed out) can be mixed in at this stage for variety.

Mix well. Stir in egg yolks one at a time. Beat whites until soft peaks form and gently fold into cheese sauce with a metal spoon. Don't over-mix.

Pour into greased 30 x 25cm lamington tin lined with greaseproof paper. Bake in moderate oven for 15 minutes or until puffed and lightly browned. (If pressed gently with finger, roulade should bounce into shape again.)

Turn out onto a tea towel. Peel paper off carefully and gently roll up with the aid of the towel. Leave for 5 minutes and then unroll.

Spread with filling, not quite covering one end to allow mixture not to come out. Roll up.

Put onto tray again and sprinkle with Parmesan. Garnish top with walnut halves and heat at high temperature for about 15 minutes.

Serves 6

Step 1: *Pour into a greased and lined lamington tin*

Walnut and avocado roulade

Step 2: *Spread filling, not quite covering one end*

Step 3: *Roll and place in tray again*

Broccoli–Avocado Lorraine

This dish is actually a quiche without the pastry.

250g broccoli
2 avocados, sliced
1 cup grated cheese
1½ cups cream
1 teaspoon dry mustard
2 pinches nutmeg
5 eggs
freshly ground pepper

Separate broccoli into small flowerettes and cook until only just tender. Grease a pie dish with butter and arrange cooked broccoli and avocado in layers.

Beat together or blend the cream, mustard, nutmeg and eggs. Pour over vegetables and top with grated cheese and fresh ground pepper.

Bake at 180°C (350°F) for about 30 minutes until set and lightly browned on top.

Note: A white sauce with lots of chopped parsley goes well with this dish.

Serves 6

Camembert–Avocado Cake

A melt-in-the-mouth savoury cake, which may be served in smaller quantities as an entrée.

1 whole Camembert
1 avocado, thinly sliced
1 beaten egg
breadcrumbs (to coat)

oil to deep fry or butter to shallow fry
flour (to coat)

Slice a very firm Camembert in three even layers. Between each layer, place overlapping slices of avocado. Form whole Camembert into a firm round.

Dip in flour, then beaten egg, then breadcrumbs and repeat coating process once again to form a thick crust.

Heat oil or butter. Cook whole Camembert cake on both sides until golden brown. During cooking, use an egg slice and the back of a spoon to gently hold the rounded edge of the Camembert cake in place while turning gently.

Top with small diced carrots cooked in a little butter and honey with a pinch of cinnamon.

Serves 2

Avocado Pasty

Filling

cubed avocado tossed
    with a little lemon juice
fresh ground pepper and
    salt to taste

This filling can be put inside any pastry (shortcrust, puff or flaky). Simply cut pastry into 15cm rounds, place filling on one half. Moisten edges and fold over to form a half-moon shape. Press edges together well.

Place on greased tray, brush with a little milk and bake at 200°C (400°F) until lightly browned.

Note: A tasty addition is the sprinkling of cheese over the filling before the pastry is sealed down.

Serves 4

Savoury Crêpe Batter

This batter recipe is basic for all main meal crêpes; it will make about 10 crêpes.

2 eggs
2 cups milk
⅔ cup plain flour
2 tablespoons oil
optional: 2 tablespoons
    ground roasted sesame
    seeds
1 teaspoon sweet paprika
    or 1 teaspoon of your
    favourite herb

Blend all ingredients in a blender. Turn machine off, stir down flour and blend again. Refrigerate 1 hour before using.

Broccoli-avocado Lorraine

Camembert–Avocado Crêpe with Caper Sauce

3 avocados, thinly sliced
3 whole Camembert
  cheeses, sliced

Sauce

60g butter
60g plain flour
150mL stock
150mL white wine
150mL cream
2 tablespoons tamari or
  soy sauce
3 tablespoons capers

Lay avocado slices over half of crêpe. Then add Camembert slices. Brown on both sides in a little butter.

Melt butter in saucepan. Add flour to make a roux. Cook for a few minutes to brown lightly. Remove from heat and slowly add stock while stirring. Add tamari and white wine.

Cook over medium heat, stirring occasionally, then add cream and capers. Cook until reasonably thick and spoon over filled, cooked crêpes.

Garnish with a sprig of parsley and a sprinkling of capers.

Serves 6

Bernoise Spinach and Avocado Loaf

250g butter
2 bunches spinach,
  shredded
handful fresh mint leaves
¼ cup chopped fresh dill
250g cream cheese
pinch or two nutmeg
4 eggs, separated
half loaf fresh bread
3 avocados, mashed with
  a little lemon juice

Soak bread in sufficient milk to make bread moist.

Mix soaked bread with beaten egg yolks, dill and nutmeg.

Sauté spinach and mint in butter until soft. Add chopped cream cheese and mix through until it starts to melt.

Purée spinach mixture in blender until smooth. Mix with soaked bread and avocados. Consistency of final mixture should be soft but not sloppy. If too moist add small amount of dry breadcrumbs.

Beat egg whites until soft peaks form; fold gently through spinach mixture.

Pour into greased 30 x 20cm dish and bake at 180°C (350°F) for about 30 minutes or until puffed and lightly browned.

Note: The loaf can be served on its own, with a spoonful of sour cream or a mushroom sauce. Garnish with dill.

Serves 8-10

Asparagus–Avocado Crêpe

Fresh asparagus is almost a must for this recipe, however the tinned variety may be used as a last resort.

18 medium-sized
  asparagus stalks
3 avocados, sliced thinly
125g Swiss cheese,
  grated
6 cooked crêpes

Bernoise spinach and avocado loaf

Trim woody ends from asparagus and cook in boiling water for about 10 minutes or in a vegetable steamer until the stalks are tender. Drain well.

Arrange, on one half of each crêpe, grated cheese, then avocado slices, then asparagus stalks.

Fold over top half and cook each side over moderate heat until insides are heated and outside of crêpe is lightly crisped.

Serves 6

CRÊPE FILLINGS:

avocado-alfalfa (top);
prawn and avocado (centre);
and oriental cashew (bottom).

Oriental Cashew Crêpe

A light crêpe meal enhanced with subtle flavours of the Orient.

⅔ cup roasted, chopped
    cashew nuts
2 cups raw chicken strips
½ cup thinly sliced
    broccoli
½ cup finely shredded
    shallots
2 large avocados, finely
    diced
1½ cups chicken stock
2 tablespoons tamari or
    soy sauce
2 tablespoons grated
    fresh root ginger
2 tablespoons arrowroot
    or cornflour
3 tablespoons oil
12 cooked crêpes
6 shallot curls
1 avocado half, sliced (for
    garnish)

Heat oil in frypan. Add chicken strips and sliced broccoli and gently toss for about 5 minutes. Add onion and stock with ginger. Cover and simmer for 10 minutes.

Remove chicken and broccoli and toss with cashew nuts and shallots. Dissolve arrowroot or cornflour in soy sauce or tamari and stir into stock mixture. Cook, stirring over medium heat until thick.

To serve, mix avocado with chicken filling and put into centre of each crêpe. Roll up and cook gently over medium heat in a little butter in frypan on both sides.

Spoon over sauce and top with a shallot curl and an avocado slice.

Serves 6

Alfalfa–Avocado Crêpe

250 g cottage cheese
2 avocados, sliced
2 loosely packed cups
  alfalfa sprouts
4 tablespoons finely
  shredded shallots
lemon juice

Combine cottage cheese and shallots. Spread over one half of cooked crêpe. Top with avocado slices and alfalfa sprouts. Fold crêpe over filling and cook gently in a little butter until filling is heated and crêpe is lightly browned and crisp on both sides.

Sprinkle a little lemon juice over when serving.

Serves 4

Prawn and Avocado Crêpe

500 g peeled, cooked
  prawns
1 cup thick tomato sauce
1 onion, sliced
1 capsicum, sliced
2 cloves garlic, crushed
dash Tabasco sauce
2 tablespoons butter
150 mL cream
4 avocados, chopped

Melt butter and cook capsicum, onion and garlic until tender. Stir in tomato sauce and tabasco sauce and cook for a few minutes. Add prawns and cream and cook until heated through.

Spoon into cooked crêpes and serve garnished with tomato slices topped with avocado purée and a prawn.

Serves 3-4

Ricotta–Avocado Flan

The flavours in this flan are similar to a pizza. This recipe makes a very nutritious meal with the addition of a leafy salad.

Pastry

200g plain flour
100g soft butter
juice of ½ lemon
¼ cup water

Cut butter into flour with a long-bladed knife and then rub in with fingertips to resemble breadcrumbs. Mix lemon juice and water together and mix into flour with a spoon until pastry forms a ball.

Wrap in plastic and refrigerate 1 hour before using. (The quantities of liquid may vary slightly depending on whether you use wholemeal or white flour.)

Filling

500g ricotta cheese
3 large eggs, beaten
3 avocados, sliced
⅛ teaspoon nutmeg
1 large onion, chopped
1 capsicum, finely
    chopped
2 zucchini, grated
2 tomatoes, chopped
2 tablespoons tomato
    paste
2 tablespoons butter
¼ cup fresh basil or 1
    teaspoon dried basil
2 cups grated cheese

Beat ricotta with eggs and nutmeg. Cook onion, capsicum and zucchini in butter for 10 minutes. Then add basil, tomatoes and tomato paste and cook until tomatoes are well cooked and mixture is of a sauce-like consistency.

To assemble, roll out pastry and line a greased pie dish with it. Put a thin layer of ricotta mixture over the bottom of the pastry, then a layer of the tomato and vegetable mixture, followed by a layer of avocado slices and, lastly, a layer of grated cheese.

Repeat all the layers again if you have the room, ending with grated cheese.

Bake at 180°C (350°F) for about 30 minutes.

Note: You can serve this flan hot or at room temperature.

Serves 8-10

Corn and Avocado Tacos

Tacos, using this delicious avocado-based filling, make a perfect lunch or light dinner.

corn kernels, scraped
   from 3 cobs or 1 x
   small can corn kernels
3 small avocados,
   chopped
30 g butter
2 medium onions, finely
   chopped

2 cloves garlic, crushed
1/2 teaspoon dried basil
1 cup cooked red kidney
   beans
1 cup grated cheese
1 cup sour cream
paprika and a tomato, for
   the garnish

Melt butter in a frypan. Cook onions, garlic and basil for 5 minutes over a moderate heat. Add corn and cook further 5 minutes. Toss through cooked kidney beans until hot and then arrange the chopped avocado over the mixture. Place lid on frypan and turn off heat. Leave for a few minutes, to allow avocado to warm. Toss mixture gently and fill each taco just over half way, topping with grated cheese and some sour cream. Sprinkle paprika over sour cream and garnish with a tomato slice when serving.

Serves 4-6

Lebanese Avocado-Cauliflower

The cauliflower is served whole for a spectacular presentation.

1 medium cauliflower
2 avocados
1 clove garlic
1 cup tahini paste
1/2 cup lemon juice

1/2 teaspoon salt
1/2 cup chopped parsley
water or stock
1/2 cup roasted pine nuts

Steam or boil whole cauliflower in large saucepan till tender.

Blend (in blender) garlic, salt and lemon juice until a smooth purée. Then add tahini paste, chopped avocados and enough water or stock to make a reasonably thick sauce.

Gently warm the sauce in a saucepan until hot and pour over whole hot cauliflower placed on a serving platter.

Garnish with roasted pine nuts and place in centre of dinner table for an impressive dish.

Serves 4

Garden Avocado Mornay

A melt-in-the-mouth Mornay to eat with a light salad. Any combination of vegetables can be used.

2 chopped avocados
1 large potato, cooked
   and sliced
2 cobs corn, cooked and
   scraped or 1/2 small can
   of corn kernels
1/2 cup chopped cooked
   pumpkin
1/2 cup fresh peas,
   cooked
parsley to garnish

Toss with prepared Mornay Sauce and serve immediately or put into greased baking dish and heat through in oven until lightly browned on top.

Mornay Sauce

3 cups milk
1 small onion, sliced
3 bay leaves
1 teaspoon whole dried
   thyme
pinch nutmeg
5 tablespoons butter
1/2 cup plain flour
2/3 cup grated cheese
1/2 cup grated Parmesan
   cheese
freshly ground pepper

Infuse milk with onion, bay leaves and thyme over moderate heat. Don't boil.

Remove from heat and stand for 15 minutes with a lid on. Strain. Melt butter and stir in flour to form a roux. Cook 3 minutes. Remove from heat and slowly stir in strained milk.

Mix until smooth and return to heat, stirring until sauce thickens. Beat with rotary beater to smooth sauce out. Add cheeses and stir until melted.

Serves 4

Lebanese avocado-cauliflower

SALADS, SNACKS' AND OTHER SURPRISES

Avocado goes well with virtually any salad combination — and in this chapter there are some special
ones. The pale yellowy-green of the avocado complements the contrasting colours of other fruits and
vegetables, such as beetroot and orange, and makes
arranging an avocado salad a joy for the cook.

Not all sauces appear in this section, as some follow
related individual recipes throughout the book. A
sweet avocado sauce is tasty to eat and a visual delight
when served with a fruit salad, and the savoury avocado sauces are particularly good with seafood.

As well as a range of snacks there are some unusual
drink combinations — perfect for a nourishing breakfast, a lunch when time is short or a refreshing break
at any time of day.

Sweet and savoury recipes using avocados provide
easily digestible and highly nutritious meals for babies.
These dishes can be given to babies as a first intro-
duction to solids and will also be enjoyed by older
children.

Avocado cream sauce
Recipe page 68

Tropical Superwhip

1 avocado, chopped
1 banana, chopped
¼ cup pawpaw,
　chopped
2 teaspoons honey
2 teaspoons desiccated
　coconut
6 fresh mint leaves
600 mL orange juice or
　milk

Blend all ingredients and serve in very tall glasses, with a slice of kiwi fruit on the side of the glass. Decorate with a cocktail umbrella or fancy straw.

Serves 4

Opposite:
(left to right)
Banannie avocado whip,
Tropical superwhip and
Orange avocado and yoghurt
whip.

Egg, avocado and beet salad

Egg, Avocado and Beet Salad

500 g cooked beetroot,
　thinly sliced into
　julienne strips
4 hard-boiled eggs,
chopped carefully into
　chunks
2 avocados, finely sliced

Arrange beetroot strips on a plate, avocado on top and chopped egg on top of that. Spoon over dressing.

Dressing

1 tablespoon French
　mustard
3 tablespoons wine
　vinegar
½ cup olive oil
freshly ground pepper
salt to taste
1 tablespoon finely
　chopped onion

Combine all ingredients in a bowl and beat with a fork or whisk until well mixed.

Note: Reserve a little of the cooked egg white which can be very finely chopped and sprinkled over the finished salad. Garnish with a spray of fresh dill if desired.

Serves 4

Wined Avocado Spread

A deliciously creamy spread that can be served with Melba toast or crackers after a meal, as an entree or a snack.

2 x 150g tins Camembert
cheese
250g avocados
1 cup dry white wine
few drops Tabasco sauce
160g ground, lightly
roasted almonds

Chop Camembert cheese coarsely and marinate with wine. Mash a little. Allow to stand overnight and strain the next day. The liquid remaining could be used to make a white wine sauce.

Mash Camembert with avocado until smooth and creamy (an electric mixer does this well). Refrigerate 10 minutes or so, until firm enough to mould.

This can now be placed into little pots and sprinkled with ground nuts, or moulded into empty avocado shells, and taken out carefully when very well chilled and firm.

The moulded spread can be rolled in the ground almonds.

Note: This spread is delightful when served with a selection of crudités.

Serves 10-12

Minted Orange and Avocado Salad

A salad which is so refreshing you could eat it in the morning for breakfast.

2 avocados, finely sliced
   or shredded
2 oranges, peeled and
   segmented
4 slices fresh pineapple
4 lettuce or curly endive
   leaves
2 tablespoons roasted
   chopped hazelnuts

Place pineapple slices on lettuce leaves. Arrange avocado slices and orange segments over pineapple.

Spoon over orange dressing and garnish with hazelnuts, and orange and chive shreds.

Dressing

125g cream cheese
juice of 2 oranges, or
   vary to make dressing
   required thickness
a handful fresh mint
Garnish:
Orange and chive shreds

Blend cream cheese, orange juice and mint in blender until of good consistency or beat with fork until smooth. Chill before serving.

Serves 4

Nordic Avocado-Pear Salad

Very simple and quick to prepare.

2 avocados, sliced
2 large pears (peeled only
   if skin isn't in good
   condition) and finely
   sliced
4 large slices Jarlsberg
   cheese, cut in julienne
   shreds
4 lettuce leaves
2 tablespoons pecan
   nuts, halved

Arrange avocado, pear and cheese slices attractively on lettuce leaf and top with dressing. Sprinkle with a little paprika or poppy seeds to garnish and finish with a sprinkling of pecan nuts.

Dressing

1 tablespoon honey
1 tablespoon lemon juice
1/2 cup sour cream
freshly ground pepper
salt to taste

Beat honey, lemon juice and seasonings with a fork in a bowl. Gradually beat in sour cream.

Serves 4

Israeli Avocado

This recipe is a version of a popular Israeli dish.

2 avocados, halved,
   peeled and sliced
   lengthways
2 oranges, peeled and in
   segments
8 strawberries

Dressing

250g cream cheese
juice of 2 lemons
handful fresh mint leaves
2 dessertspoons honey
about 1/2 cup oil

Arrange alternate slices of avocado and orange on a plate or use your own imaginative presentation.

   Garnish with strawberries and fresh mint leaves and serve dressing separately in a bowl or jug.

Serves 4

Rice and Avocado Salad

An exotic blend of sweet and sour flavours, delightful if eaten on its own (or with other salads) or with a curry-flavoured main dish.

2 cups cooked brown rice
1 small cucumber,
   chopped
2 small avocados,
   chopped
2 bananas, halved and
   sliced
2 tablespoons raisins
   soaked in juice of 1/2
   orange for 30 minutes
2 tablespoons chopped
   brazil nuts
1/2 green and red
   capsicum, finely
   shredded

Mix together rice, cucumber, raisins, brazil nuts and capsicum. Lastly, toss in avocado and banana. Mix in dressing and serve well chilled.

Dressing

4 tablespoons olive oil
1 1/2 tablespoons lemon
   juice
1 tablespoon grated
   orange rind
1/4 teaspoon ground
   coriander
1/4 teaspoon ground
   cumin
1 tablespoon honey
freshly ground pepper
salt to taste

Shake all ingredients together in a jar and allow to marinate for at least 30 minutes or, ideally, overnight before using. Garnish with a brilliantly coloured tropical flower.

   Note: Allow enough time for the flavour of the dressing to penetrate into the salad.

Serves 4

Rice and avocado salad

Nordic avocado pear salad
Recipe page 62

Prawn–Avocado Salad Bowl

Serve this in a flat bowl as a summer lunch, or in a smaller bowl as a delicious entrée. Prepare the dressing an hour before.

1 kg cooked prawns
2 avocados, formed into
   balls with a melon
   baller
2 medium carrots, cut
   into julienne strips
2 celery stalks, cut into
   julienne strips
1 small Chinese cabbage,
   finely shredded
1 shallot, finely shredded

Toss all ingredients together with dressing; chill for a little while before serving. Sprinkle with shredded shallot.

Dressing

juice of 1 lemon
1 clove garlic, crushed
1 cup salad oil
½ bunch finely chopped
   shallots
freshly ground pepper
salt to taste
1 tablespoon roasted
   sesame seeds

Shake all ingredients in a jar and allow to stand for 1 hour before using.
   Sprinkle salad with sesame seeds and serve on a bed of curly endive, if desired.

Serves 4

Prawn-avocado salad bowl

Lemon-stuffed Avocado Eggs

1 avocado, mashed
juice of 1 lemon
8 hard-boiled eggs,
  halved and shelled
1/4 teaspoon Dijon
  mustard
fresh ground pepper
1/4 teaspoon tarragon

Garnish

avocado julienne strips
coarsely cracked black
  peppercorns

Mash avocado with egg yolks and lemon juice. Mix through mustard, tarragon and seasonings. Mixture should be smooth and creamy.

Pile into egg cavities and smooth over surface or decorate filling by piping through a cake decorator's bag. Garnish with avocado strips and a sprinkling of coarsely cracked black peppercorns. Serve on a bed of finely shredded red cabbage.

Serves 4

Lemon-stuffed avocado eggs

Step 1: Cut the top off each tomato and remove pulp

Guacamole-stuffed Tomatoes

An exciting use for a well-known filling.

4 large tomatoes
2 small avocados,
  mashed
1/3 cup lemon juice
1 clove garlic, crushed
freshly ground pepper
salt to taste
1 tablespoon finely
  chopped green chillies
  or pinch or two of chilli
  powder
2 tablespoons chopped
  parsley
1/2 teaspoon coriander
  powder
several black olives

Cut off the top of each tomato. Cut around inside edge of tomato to remove pulp from the sides, being careful not to damage the skin. Scoop out tomato pulp with a teaspoon.

Mix avocados with remaining ingredients. Beat with a fork until well mixed and smooth. Add half of the chopped tomato pulp to avocado mixture. Pile back into tomato shells. Garnish with olives.

Note: This recipe makes a superb accompaniment to most main dishes and any salad. Cherry tomatoes can be substituted for use as an hors d'oeuvre.

Serves 4

Guacamole-stuffed tomatoes

Step 2: Mix avocados with remaining ingredients

Step 3: Pile back into tomato shells, with a garnish of olives

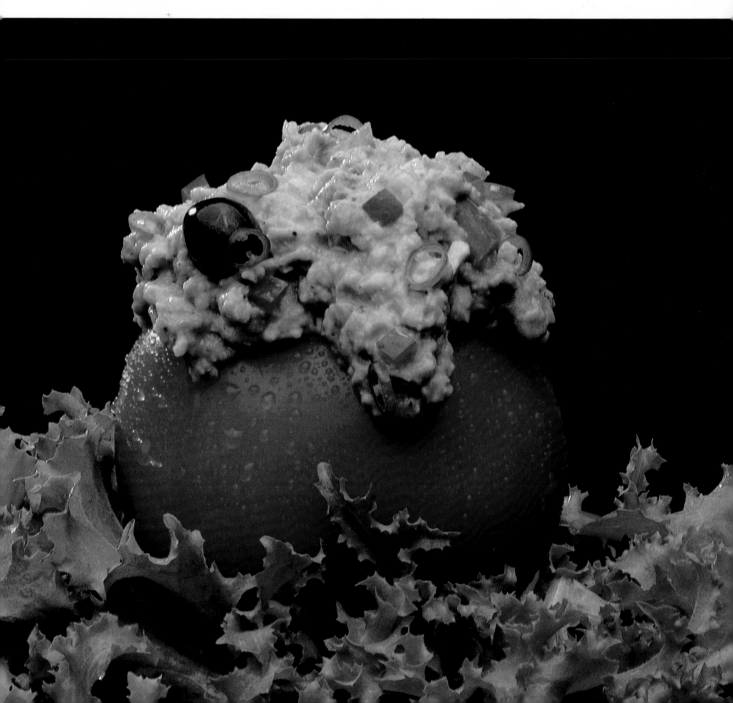

Avocado cream sauce

Alligator Pear Fruit Sauce

Alligator Pear was the original name for the avocado.

1 avocado
1 dessertspoon honey
juice of 1 orange

Blend all ingredients in a blender until smooth. Cream can be folded through this or a banana can be added.
  Note: Serve this recipe over fruit salad tossed in coconut.

Serves 2

Avocado Cream Sauce

Especially delicious served over a salad of luscious tropical fruits.

1 avocado
2 teaspoons honey
300 mL cream

Blend until smooth and thick in a blender or food processor.
  Note: Weight-conscious people can substitute cottage cheese or natural yoghurt for the cream.

Serves 2

Egg and Avocado Sauce

A creamy egg sauce, delightful with pasta.

1 large avocado,
    chopped
2 hard-boiled eggs,
    chopped
2 cups milk
50g butter
2 tablespoons plain flour

½ teaspoon prepared
    mustard
freshly ground pepper
salt to taste
3 tablespoons finely
    chopped chives

Blend milk with avocado until smooth. Melt butter and stir in flour, mustard and seasonings. Add avocado milk and stir constantly until sauce thickens. Reduce heat and simmer for a few minutes, adding chopped eggs and chives.

Note: Tuna complements this sauce well; 150g can be added with the eggs and chives.

If serving with pasta, sprinkle some grated parmesan cheese on top.

Serves 4

Avocado Fish Sauce

Any crumbed fish fillets or grilled fish will be enhanced by this sauce.

1 large avocado, mashed
1 clove garlic, crushed
1 tablespoon butter
100mL cream
2 teaspoons lemon juice

Cook crushed garlic in butter for a few minutes, stirring, until golden brown. Stir in mashed avocado, cream and lemon juice and heat through. Don't allow to boil.

Note: You can reheat this sauce within a period of about two hours.

Serves 2

Avocado fish sauce — a wonderful topping for any crumbed or grilled fish dish.

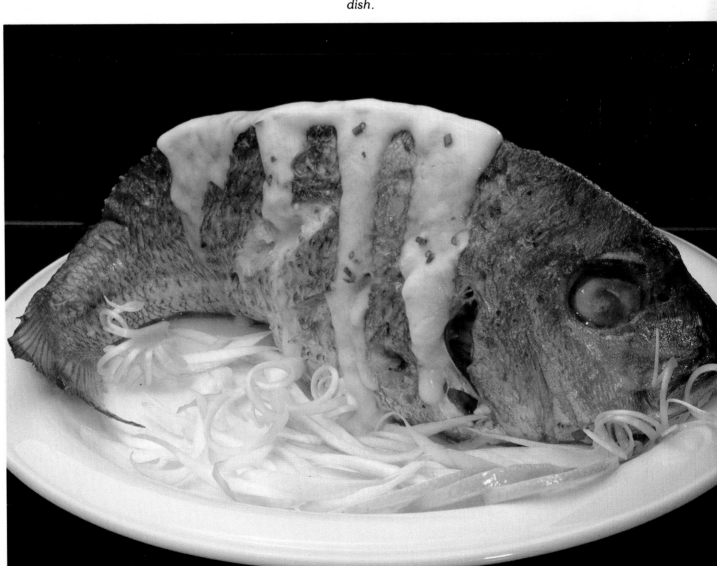

Oriental Stuffed Avocado

A sentimental favourite of mine; it won an award and set me on the road to writing this book.

1 large avocado, halved
    and seeded
1 tablespoon chopped
    parsley
1 tablespoon finely
    shredded shallots
2 tablespoons finely
    chopped celery
3 tablespoons alfalfa
    sprouts or Chinese
    mung bean sprouts

Toss together the parsley, celery, shallots and sprouts. Spoon this into cavity of avocado, piling high.

Cover lightly with sauce and sprinkle with chopped toasted almonds to serve.

Sauce

1 tablespoon freshly
    grated ginger
1 clove garlic, crushed
60 g tamari or soy sauce
enough honey to
    sweeten to taste (about
    1 tablespoon)

Put all ingredients in blender and blend until smooth. Garnish with toasted almonds, slivered or finely chopped.

Note: The flavour of the sauce improves if made the day before; the full aroma of the ginger comes out.

Serves 2

Oriental stuffed avocado — always sure to please, and the inspiration for this book.

Almond–Avocado Milk

1 avocado, chopped
2 teaspoons honey
4 teaspoons ground raw
    almonds
1 teaspoon vanilla
    essence
about 600 mL milk
nutmeg to garnish

Blend the milk, ground almonds, honey and vanilla for a couple of minutes in a blender.

With blender still in motion, drop chopped avocado through hole in lid and blend until smooth. The whip should be thick, but of pouring consistency (adjust with more milk).

Sprinkle with nutmeg to serve.

Serves 4

Orange Avocado and Yoghurt Whip

1 avocado, chopped
    coarsely
juice of 2 oranges
1 dessertspoon honey
pinch cinnamon
2 dessertspoons natural
    yoghurt

Blend all ingredients and serve with crushed ice and an orange twist on the side of the glass.

Serves 2

Emerald Milk Whip

½ avocado, chopped
1 teaspoon honey
300 mL milk
2 scoops natural vanilla
    ice-cream
cinnamon to garnish

Blend all ingredients in blender and serve sprinkled with cinnamon.

Serves 2

Avocado 'Baby' Sweet

Any baby will love this treat. It's good for older children too.

1/4 medium avocado
2 dates, soaked overnight
  in water
1/2 banana
1 teaspoon finely ground
  sunflower seeds

Blend all ingredients in a blender or food processor until well combined. Add a little orange juice or water if too thick.

Serves 1

Banannie Avocado Whip

1 large avocado,
  chopped
1 banana, chopped
2 teaspoons honey
1 teaspoon vanilla
  essence
3 glasses of milk

Blend all ingredients in a blender until smooth and thick. Sprinkle with a little nutmeg to serve.

Serves 4

Avocado 'Baby' Savoury

Once a baby is ready for solids, avocados provide an excellent source of protein, vitamins and minerals.

1 small carrot, grated
1 tablespoon alfalfa
  sprouts
1 very small lettuce leaf
1/4 medium avocado

sprig parsley
juice of 1 small orange
1 teaspoon tahini paste or
  peanut paste

Blend carrot, sprouts, lettuce, orange juice until well puréed, stirring down occasionally.

Add avocado and tahini or peanut paste and parsley. Purée again until smooth.

Serves 1

72

Avocado Stuffed Rolls

These rolls make a great lunch or snack.

4 hard-boiled eggs,
  chopped
2 avocados, chopped
3/4 cup grated cheese
2 tablespoons chopped
  capsicum
2 tablespoons finely
  chopped parsley
2 tablespoons tomato
  paste
2 tablespoons salad oil
4 large round
  wholewheat bread rolls

Cut bread rolls in half. Scoop out insides, leaving a good crust. Mix all ingredients and stuff mix into roll cavity. Replace tops and wrap in foil.

Bake in moderate oven 180°C (350°F) for about 30 minutes.

Serves 4

Avocado Salad Dressing

1 avocado
1/4 cup lemon juice
1/2 teaspoon salt
1/2 teaspoon freshly
  ground pepper
1/2 cup salad oil

1 tablespoon wine
  vinegar or apple cider
  vinegar
2 egg yolks
1 tablespoon chopped
  onion

Blend egg yolks, lemon juice, salt and pepper, vinegar and onion. Then add avocado while blender is in motion.

Add oil slowly until thick, like mayonnaise. If all of the oil can't be added, add a little water and then the remaining oil.

Your favourite herbs can be added to this dressing (chives, tarragon, parsley, dill or basil go very well).

Note: These quantities should yield 1 1/2 cups of dressing.

Avocado salad dressing

Avocado stuffed rolls
Recipe page 72

DESSERTS

It may be difficult to imagine natural green desserts, but — apart from the spectacular colour of the avocado, which can be used to great effect to decorate, garnish or blend with other ingredients — the texture lends itself superbly to sweet dishes.

Included in this section are ice-creams, sorbets, cheesecakes, soufflés, pancakes and gâteaux. Banana is an excellent fruit to combine with avocado, both in texture and flavour. This combination has been used in the Banavo Pancake and suggested for the Avocado Ice-Cream.

The subtle flavour of the avocado seems to be retained quite well in cooked desserts, such as the Avocado Passionfruit and Yoghurt Flan and the Custard and Avocado Tart. As previously mentioned, the uncooked avocado loses its colour and browns very easily and this should be borne in mind when preparing desserts such as the Date Avocado Tango and the Green Gâteau.

Custard and avocado tart.
Recipe page 82

Date–Avocado Tango

This dish is similar to a mousse, but with more 'goodies'.

2 avocados, mashed
150 mL whipped cream
2 tablespoons honey
juice of 1 orange
rind of 1 orange
4 tablespoons chopped
  dates
2 egg whites, stiffly
  beaten

Mix well avocado, honey, orange juice, rind and dates. Fold whipped cream through (stiffly) and then egg whites (gently) with a metal spoon.

Serve in individual bowls and garnish with very thin strips of orange rind (cooked in honey and water-syrup until soft).

Decorate with more whipped cream around the edges if desired.

Serves 4

Date-avocado tango

Avocado Bavarois

1 cup milk
2.5 cm piece vanilla bean,
  split
1 sachet gelatine, or 1
  tablespoon agar-agar,
  cooked in ¼ cup water
2 tablespoons cold water
125 g sugar
4 egg yolks

1 cup cream, whipped
  stiffly
1 avocado, mashed with
  1 tablespoon honey
  and a squeeze lemon
  juice
whipped cream to
  garnish

Scald milk with vanilla bean and set aside to infuse for 30 minutes. Soften gelatine in cold water. Beat egg yolks with sugar until pale yellow. Pour milk over egg mixture, beating constantly.

Cook over very low heat or in double boiler until thick. Do not boil. Remove vanilla bean. Add softened gelatine to stiffly whipped cream. Mash avocado with honey and lemon juice. Cool.

To assemble, spoon cooled custard to just below halfway in serving glass or dish. Then add layer of avocado mashed with honey and juice and top off with remaining custard.

Garnish with stiffly whipped cream and a strawberry or tiny macaroons.

Serves 3-4

Almondine Avocado Meringue

A dessert lover's delight, combining a beautiful almond meringue with sweetened avocado purée and cream, and set off with melted chocolate on top.

1 cup roasted almonds,
   finely chopped or
   ground
4 egg whites
1 cup fine raw sugar
1¼ cups cream, stiffly
   whipped
1 teaspoon vanilla
   essence
2 avocados, mashed,
   with 2 tablespoons
   honey
50g dark chocolate,
   melted in double boiler

Line two baking trays with foil. Draw a 15 cm ring on each.

Whisk egg whites until very stiff and holding peaks. Whisk in 1 tablespoon of sugar, then fold in remaining sugar with a metal spoon.

Sprinkle over ¾ cup of roasted almonds and very quickly cut them into the meringue.

Spoon half of the mixture on to the prepared tray, mounding up the sides a little, and the other half onto the other tray.

The meringue, which will go on top to assemble, should be peaked a little.

Bake at 160°C (310°F) for 35 to 40 minutes or until firm and lightly golden.

Peel off foil and replace, upside down, into oven to cool with door open slightly.

To assemble, sandwich the meringue together with a layer of whipped cream and a layer of avocado purée. Decorate the top of the meringue with melted chocolate and refrigerate about ½ hour before serving.

Serves 6-8

Step 1: *Revolve dishes to coat sides and base with caramel*

Step 2: *Pour milk over egg and avocado mixture*

Step 3: *Pour custard into dishes prior to baking*

North Coast Crème Caramel

A variation to a traditional dessert — an avocado touch served with fruits of the North Coast. This recipe can be made a day ahead.

Caramel

¾ cup raw sugar
1 cup water

Stir sugar and water over low heat until sugar dissolves. Bring to boil, without stirring, and cook until a rich golden brown. Don't stir.

Pour caramel evenly into individual soufflé dishes and, working very fast, revolve dishes in order to coat sides and base.

Use an oven glove as dishes become quite hot when coating with caramel.

Custard

2 cups milk
1½ cups mashed avocado
¼ cup raw sugar

4 eggs
2 egg yolks
1 teaspoon vanilla essence or vanilla bean
300 mL cream, whipped

Place eggs, egg yolks, vanilla and sugar in a bowl and beat together lightly. Beat in mashed avocado until smooth and creamy.

Heat milk and bring to just below boiling point. (If using vanilla bean, heat bean with milk.) Cool 10 minutes and add vanilla essence.

Pour milk over egg and avocado mixture, stirring constantly. Strain if any large lumps occur.

Place caramel-lined dishes in a baking tray. Add water to tray so that it is half-way up sides of dishes. Pour in custard and bake in 160°C (310°F) oven for about 30 to 35 minutes or until custard is set.

Cover each dish with foil and refrigerate several hours before serving.

Topping

¼ avocado, finely sliced
½ mango, finely diced
½ kiwi fruit, finely sliced

½ large banana, finely sliced
1 teaspoon finely sliced pawpaw

Combine fruit together.

To serve, ease custard away from sides of dish with fingers. Turn out onto individual small plates or saucers. Decorate with whipped cream piped around edge of custard. Fill centre with colourful array of chopped fruits.   Serves 6

Chocolate–Avocado Swirl

1 large avocado
1 teaspoon vanilla
 essence
2 teaspoons honey
1 cup whipped cream
40 g dark chocolate,
 melted
30 g dark chocolate curls

Mash avocado with vanilla and honey. Fold through whipped cream. Slowly pour cooled, melted chocolate into avocado cream. Stir in slightly so as to give a streaky look.

Put into tall parfait glasses or bowls and garnish with curls.

Note: To accentuate the chocolate swirl, use a piping bag with a very fine attachment and make a spiral design on the inside of the glass. Allow to set and gently spoon in avocado mixture.

Serves 2

Chocolate avocado swirl

Lemon–Avocado Soufflé

A rich, beautiful and tasty end to a meal.

200 g raw sugar
2 lemons
4 egg yolks
6 egg whites
3 avocados

2 tablespoons gelatine or
 agar-agar
300 mL whipped cream
avocado slices and a
 lemon twist to garnish

Beat egg yolks and sugar together. Grate rinds of lemons and squeeze the juice. Add rind and 6 tablespoons of lemon juice to egg yolks, beating constantly.

Soften gelatine in 6 tablespoons water and heat until it is liquid. Do the same if using agar-agar. Cool slightly.

Whip cream and beat into mashed avocados. Then stir into lemon and egg mixture.

Stir in gelatine and continue until it begins to thicken.

Beat egg whites until soft peaks form. Fold into lemon and avocado mixture.

Spoon carefully into a soufflé dish or tall parfait glasses and chill until set.

Note: This soufflé can be served with extra whipped cream and garnished with avocado slices, a lemon twist and a sprig of mint.

Serves 10

Green-with-Envy Cheesecake

Cheesecake is loved by all, and with this avocado filling it will be even more popular.

2 cups fine biscuit crumbs
1/2 cup melted butter
3 tablespoons raw sugar
3 avocados
500g cream cheese
3 eggs
1 cup cream
1 teaspoon vanilla
    essence
1/2 teaspoon cinnamon
1/4 cup brandy
1 cup honey or raw sugar
whipped cream to
    garnish and kiwi fruit
    slices

Mix biscuit crumbs with the melted butter and sugar, working it together with your fingers. Press into well-greased spring-form tin and, using a masher, make a flat, smooth crust.

Beat cream cheese with avocados, cream, eggs, honey or sugar until smooth. This can be done in a blender, electric mixer or food processor. Add cinnamon, vanilla and brandy.

Pour mixture into prepared spring-form pan and bake at 160°C (310°F) for about 1 hour.

Cool, refrigerate and garnish with whipped cream and kiwi fruit before serving.

Serves 12

Green-with-envy cheesecake

Custard and Avocado Tart

A tart with a rich pastry that can be served slightly warm or chilled.

Pastry

60g butter
125g plain flour
30g raw sugar
1 whole egg
2 egg yolks

Cut butter into flour and mix with fingertips until it develops a sandy texture. Mix egg yolks and egg with sugar and combine with flour mix. Form into a ball and refrigerate 30 minutes before using.

Grease a 20cm pie dish and press pastry evenly in with fingertips over the bottom and sides. (This pastry has a very crumbly consistency and cannot be rolled.)

Prick all over with a fork and bake at 200°C (400°F) for only 5 minutes. Pour in filling and bake at 180°C (350°F) for 20 to 30 minutes or until set.

Serve at room temperature with whipped cream or serve cold.

Filling

1 cup milk
1 cup cream
125g raw sugar or honey
2 teaspoons vanilla
  essence
4 eggs, separated
1 large avocado (or 2
  medium-sized)

Blend all of the filling ingredients (except for the egg whites) in a blender until smooth.

Beat egg whites separately until soft peaks form; fold gently into custard with a metal spoon.

Note: The cream can be sprinkled with a little ground cinnamon or nutmeg after garnishing the tart; alternatively, decorate by dusting icing sugar over a doily placed on the tart.

Serves 6-8

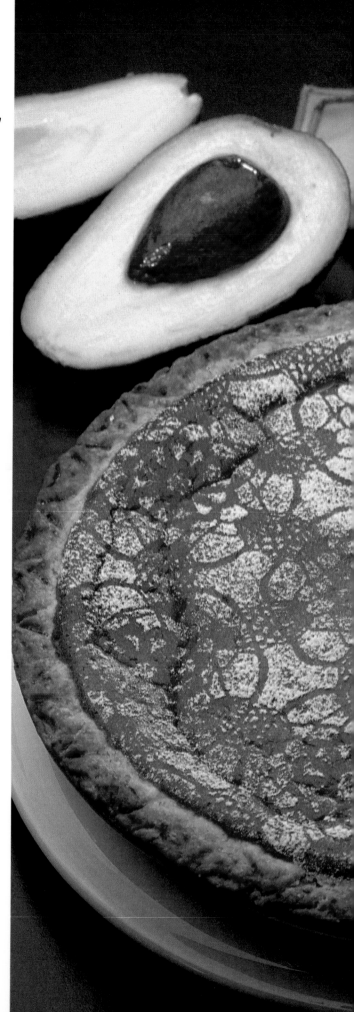

Custard and avocado tart

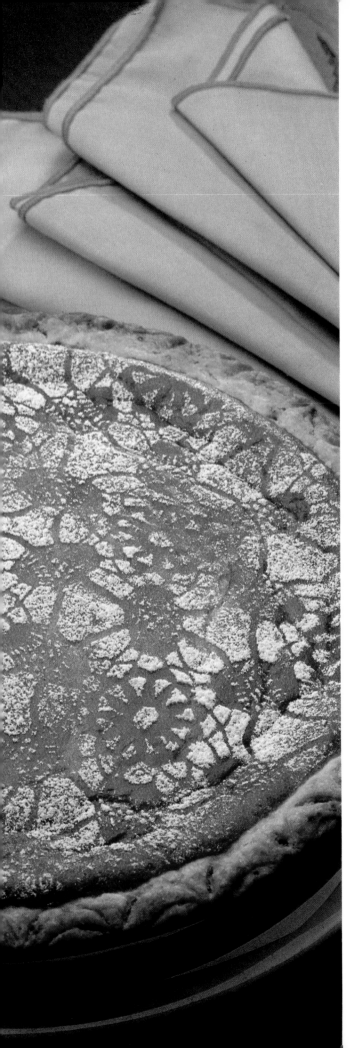

Avocado Chiffon Pie

As its name implies, this pie is light and delicate in flavour and texture.

2 cups plain flour
125g butter
1 tablespoon fine raw
    sugar
1 egg yolk
2 teaspoons lemon juice
2-3 tablespoons cold
    water

Cut butter into flour with a long-bladed knife, then rub in with fingertips. Mix through sugar. Mix egg yolk with lemon juice and water and combine with flour.

Knead lightly, wrap in plastic wrap and refrigerate 30 minutes before using.

Filling

1½ cups puréed avocado
½ cup raw sugar or
    honey
¼ cup lemon or lime
    juice
2 egg yolks, lightly beaten
3 egg whites, stiffly
    beaten
1½ tablespoons gelatine,
    dissolved in ¼ cup hot
    water or 2 tablespoons
    agar-agar, dissolved in
    ½ cup water and
    cooked in pan for 5
    minutes
¼ cup fine raw sugar

Place egg yolks, honey or sugar in double boiler and heat until sugar dissolves or honey is well combined. Quickly stir into avocado purée.

Add softened gelatine or agar-agar, stirring quickly and well, and then stir in lemon or lime juice.

Chill until partially set, checking every 10 minutes or so. Roll out pastry and line a 20cm flan dish. Bake 'blind'. Cool. Beat the ¼ cup fine raw sugar into beaten egg whites.

Fold egg whites into avocado custard mixture. Pour into prepared pastry and swirl filling into small peaks.

Refrigerate for at least 2 hours before serving.

Note: It is important to use freshly ripened avocados with this dish to prevent the possibility of discoloration.

Serves 8

Passionfruit avocado and yoghurt flan

Passionfruit Avocado and Yoghurt Flan

A highly nutritious dish that keeps well.

Pastry

200g plain flour
50g desiccated coconut
1 tablespoon sugar

125g soft butter
apple juice or water to
moisten

Mix flour, coconut and sugar. Cut in butter with long-bladed knife and rub with fingertips until it resembles breadcrumbs. Add enough apple juice or water to make dough come together.

Form a ball, wrap in plastic and refrigerate for at least 1 hour before using.

Filling

3 eggs
5 tablespoons honey
1 teaspoon vanilla
1½ cups natural yoghurt

4 large passionfruit
2 large avocados,
mashed

Beat eggs, honey, vanilla and yoghurt. Mix mashed avocados and passionfruit pulp into egg mix.

Pour into prepared pastry case and bake at 180°C (350°F) for about 30 minutes until just set.

Cool and serve with whipped cream, extra passionfruit sprinkled with cinnamon, or nutmeg.

Serves 8–10

Zabaglione Cream Squares with Avocado

Zabaglione is a widely loved Italian dessert. The addition of avocado transforms these pastry squares into something superb.

250g puff pastry
2 avocados, very thinly
sliced

Roll pastry out to a 23cm square. Cut into 9 squares. Bake on a greased tray at 200°C (400°F) for 10 minutes or until lightly browned.

Cool on a wire rack.

Zabaglione Cream

3 egg yolks
2 tablespoons raw sugar
3 tablespoons Marsala
wine

1 cup stiffly whipped
cream

Whisk all ingredients in a double boiler or heatproof bowl over simmering water. Continue whisking until mixture becomes frothy and thick and rises. Cool.

Fold through whipped cream. Refrigerate for 1 hour before using.

To serve, carefully cut each square of pastry in half. Pipe or spread the Zabaglione cream onto the bottom square and decorate with thinly sliced avocado. Replace pastry top. Finely chopped roasted almonds or hazelnuts can be sprinkled over the avocado before replacing the lid.

Note: Fruit juice can be substituted for the Marsala wine. Serves 9

Step 1: *Cut the pastry into squares*

Zabaglione cream squares with avocado

Step 2: *Whisk until mixture becomes frothy, thick and rises*

Step 3: *Cut squares into halves, pipe cream onto bottom half*

Creamed Avocado Puffs

Everyone loves cream puffs, and with avocado filling they simply melt in the mouth.

Puff Mixture

1 cup water
3½ tablespoons butter,
*   cut in small pieces*
1 tablespoon raw sugar
1 cup sifted plain flour
4 eggs

Place water, butter and sugar in pan and stir to completely melt butter. Bring to boil and remove from heat. Add flour all at once and stir vigorously. Reheat mixture for 2 minutes until the dough forms a ball.

Remove from heat and beat each egg well into mixture, one at a time. Butter and flour oven trays and, using 2 spoons, form balls about the size of an egg. Place 8 cm apart on tray.

Bake at 200°C (400°F) for 20 minutes or until puffed and golden brown.

Filling

⅔ cup raw sugar
5 egg yolks
⅔ cup plain flour
1½ cups milk
1 teaspoon vanilla
*   essence*
2 cups chopped avocado
a little Creme de Menthe
*   may be added*
1 cup whipped cream
*   sweetened with a little*
*   honey*

Beat sugar and yolks until thick and lemon coloured. Beat in flour. Heat milk and add to egg, sugar and flour mixture. Cook over moderate heat, stirring, to form a thick custard. Cool.

Slice top of each puff. Fill with cooled custard and remaining space with avocado cream. Garnish with avocado slices and finely sliced strawberries. Replace cream puff lid. Dust with sifted icing sugar before serving.

Serves 8

Creamed avocado puffs —
a wonderful dessert or
afternoon snack.

Green Gâteau

*Green gâteau —
a truly delicious treat
for adventurous chefs.*

Be adventurous! Try this delicate sponge, layered and iced in 'this year's' colour.

*6 egg yolks
8 egg whites, beaten stiff
   but not dry
1 cup fine raw sugar
   (finely ground in a
   blender)*

*3 tablespoons cold water
1 teaspoon vanilla
   essence
grated rind of 1 lemon
1 tablespoon lemon juice
1½ cups plain
   wholemeal flour*

Beat yolks until light and creamy. Add sugar, 2 tablespoons at a time, beating constantly. Beat until sugar is well combined. Add water, 1 tablespoon at a time. Then add rind and juice with vanilla.

Beat whites and place on top of mixture. Sift flour on top. Carefully fold it all together with a large metal spoon until combined. Spoon into greased 25 cm cake tin or spring-form tin and bake at 170°C (325°F) for about 1 hour (or until a skewer inserted in centre comes out clean).

Run a knife around edge and gently empty onto cake rack to cool. Cut in half.

Filling

*150 mL stiffly whipped
   cream*

*½ large avocado
honey to sweeten*

Mash avocado and mix well into whipped cream with honey. Spread over top of the bottom half of the cut cake. Put top on.

Topping

*150 mL stiffly whipped
   cream
1 avocado*

*honey to sweeten
½ teaspoon vanilla
   essence*

Mash avocado and mix well into whipped cream with honey and vanilla. Spread over top of cake and around sides.

Garnishes

*½ cup unsalted pistachio
   nuts, finely ground
4 tablespoons unsalted
   pepitas
½ avocado, thinly sliced*

Gently press pepitas onto top or sides of cake. Decorate top of cake around the edges with ground pistachio nuts and in the centre, with the sliced avocado.

Whipped cream can be piped around edge of cake and nuts sprinkled on centre part. Optional: chocolate shavings can be sprinkled over the cake if desired.

Note: With this recipe you can substitute your favourite sponge cake and use the given filling and topping.

Serves 8-10

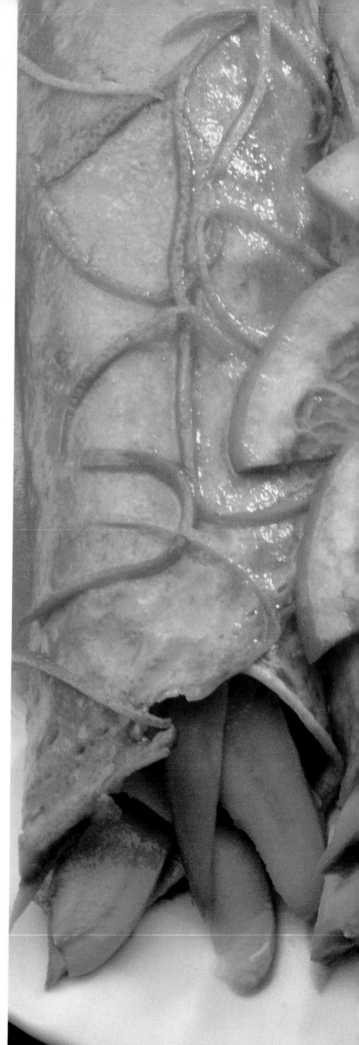

Grand Marnier avocado crêpe

French Avocado Gâteau

A choux pastry served in a spectacular symphony of greens.

2 cups water
6 tablespoons butter
2 tablespoons raw sugar
2 cups plain flour
8 eggs

Chop butter into small pieces and melt it with the water and sugar. Bring to the boil and remove from heat. Add flour all at once and stir vigorously.

Return to heat and cook further over moderate heat until pastry forms a ball.

Remove from heat and stir in eggs, one at a time, beating well.

Grease and flour 3 round pie dishes. Divide mixture equally between the dishes and spread evenly over, leaving about 2 cm between edge of pie dish and pastry. Bake at 180°C (350°F) for 20 minutes. Turn oven off and leave in further 5 minutes.

Remove from oven and cool.

Filling

2 small bunches green
* grapes, seedless*
2 cups stiffly whipped
* cream*
3 avocados, beaten with
* 4 tablespoons honey*
* until smooth and*
* creamy*

Mix avocado and honey with whipped cream until well blended. Pull grapes from stems and wash well.

To serve, spread each choux ring with avocado cream and decorate with grapes. Put the layers of choux pastry onto each other to form a gâteau. Pipe a little avocado cream around the edge of the top ring. Cut into cake wedges.

Serves 8

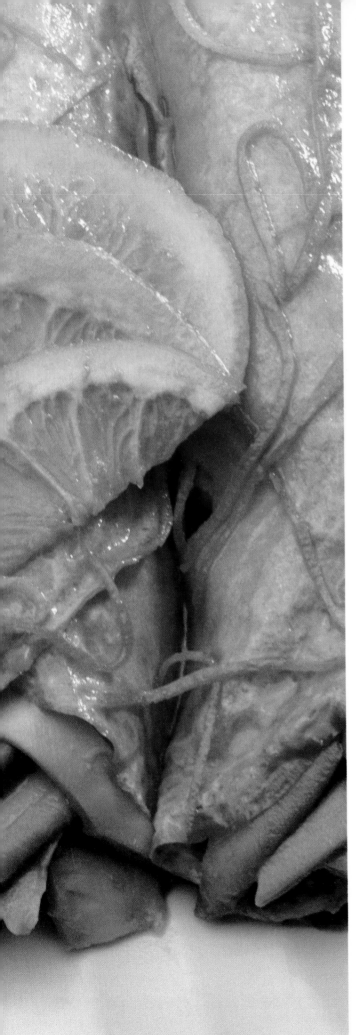

Sweet Crêpe Batter

Dessert crêpes and pancakes are always popular, and avocados make them special. The batter recipe (below) is basic for all dessert crêpes, and will make about 16 crêpes.

1¼ cups milk
1 egg, whole
1 egg yolk

1 tablespoon melted
  butter
2 tablespoons raw sugar
1 cup plain flour

Blend all ingredients in a blender. Turn off and stir down flour. Blend again and then stand in refrigerator 1 hour before using.

Use a small amount of butter to grease a heavy frypan or crêpe pan and allow pan to get fairly hot before pouring in batter.

For a crêpe, don't pour too much mixture in. Tilt the pan as you do it to shape the crêpe into a round. It is ready to turn when little bubbles appear on the surface.

Note: Unfilled crêpes or pancakes can be frozen. Allow to cool, one by one, before placing them in freezer. Once frozen, they thaw out very quickly.

Grand Marnier Avocado Crêpe

Filling

Crêpe batter as above
4 avocados, thinly sliced
whipped cream to serve

thin strips of glazed
  orange slices to garnish

Roll crêpes into cylinders with thinly sliced avocado inside.

Sauce

3 tablespoons unsalted
  butter
juice of 2 oranges
grated rind of 1 orange

2 tablespoons Grand
  Marnier
3 tablespoons raw sugar
  or honey

Heat butter in frying pan and stir in juice, rind and sugar or honey. Cook a minute or two over a gentle heat.

Add crêpe cylinders to sauce and cook gently a little on all sides. Decorate with glazed orange slices. Add Grand Marnier and light with a match. Serve, while alight, with cream in a separate dish.

Avocado Ice-Cream

Ice-cream goes with so many things and is much nicer and more nutritious if you make it yourself. The subtle taste and the green colour of the avocado makes this a truly unique ice-cream.

2 large avocados
3 cups cream
6 tablespoons honey
2 teaspoons vanilla
  essence
3 egg whites, stiffly
  beaten
3 bananas (if unavailable,
  add one extra
  avocado)

Blend avocado, cream, honey, vanilla and banana in small batches in blender until thick. Pour into ice-cream tray or container.

Beat egg whites and fold into ice-cream carefully with a metal spoon. Freeze.

Gently stir ice-cream when it is starting to freeze around the edges. Repeat twice more and then allow ice-cream to freeze.

Remove from freezer about 20 minutes before serving. Serve with fresh sliced strawberries and kiwi fruit.

Note: This recipe makes about two litres. It can be made in a commercial ice-cream maker, but I find the above method easy and successful. The key to a good consistency is ensuring that the mixture is beaten initially until thick, and also that the ice-cream is mixed as it freezes to prevent ice crystals forming.

Avocado Ice-Cream Split

This dish is a great favourite with children.

1 avocado, sliced
  lengthways into 4
  pieces
4 scoops avocado ice-
  cream (see page 00)

4-6 tablespoons pure
  maple syrup
2 tablespoons crushed
  nuts
fresh strawberries, kiwi
  fruit or cherries

Place sliced avocado along sides of long shallow glass dish. Fill centre with ice-cream scoops. Spoon over maple syrup and sprinkle with nuts. Garnish with strawberries, cherries or kiwi fruit.

Serves 2

Avocado ice-cream split

Limorange Avocado Sorbet

A sorbet with the consistency of gelato and a tangy flavour that makes it ideal in hot weather.

1½ cups avocado purée
1¼ cups fresh orange
     juice
¼ cup cream
4 tablespoons honey
juice of 1 lime or lemon
2 egg whites, stiffly
     beaten

Blend (in a blender) the avocado, cream and honey until smooth. Mix orange and lime or lemon juices together and fold through avocado purée. Gently fold through egg whites with a metal spoon.

Freeze and when almost frozen, mix and refreeze.

Note: Remove sorbet from freezer a little before needed so it can soften slightly.

Serves about 6

Strawberry and Avocado with Brandied Avocado Cream

A very simple-to-prepare dessert ideal for special occasions.

2 punnets whole   ⅓ cup fine raw sugar
   strawberries   ⅓ cup honey
4 avocados   ⅓ cup brandy
1 cup cream

Take one avocado and mash well. Whip cream, avocado and sugar in a large bowl until very thick. Stir honey and brandy together and pour into whipped avocado cream. Beat again until perfectly smooth.

Take 3 remaining avocados and cut into chunks. Gently toss avocados and strawberries together and spoon into individual serving bowls. Spoon over avocado cream and garnish with strawberry and a piece of avocado for each serving.

Alternatively, arrange layers of tossed avocado and strawberries in a parfait glass with the avocado cream. Garnish as above.

Serves 6

Sicilian Avocado Cassata

All the delicacies of true Italian cassata ice-cream made even more luscious with avocado.

First Layer

2 eggs, separated
3 dessertspoons honey
1 cup cream
1 teaspoon almond
   essence

Beat egg whites until soft peaks form. Fold in lightly beaten egg yolks. Beat cream until very stiff. Beat in honey. Add almond essence and then fold mixture into beaten eggs. Pour into 20 cm round cake tin and spread top out evenly. Freeze.

Sicilian avocado cassata

Second Layer

1 cup cream
2 egg whites
4 dessertspoons honey
1 teaspoon vanilla
 essence

2 large avocados
60g chopped toasted
 almonds
8 tablespoons mixed
 glazed fruit

Beat together cream, avocado and honey in blender until smooth and thick. Add vanilla essence. Mix in toasted almonds and glazed fruit. Beat egg whites and fold gently into cream mixture. Spread evenly over frozen first layer and freeze again.

Third Layer

1 cup cream
3 dessertspoons honey
2 eggs, separated

80g dark chocolate,
 melted in double boiler
 or heatproof bowl over
 simmering water
2 dessertspoons Marsala
 wine

Beat egg whites until soft peaks form. Beat cream until very stiff, and whip in honey and Marsala. Mix slightly cooled melted chocolate into cream and combine well. Gently fold beaten egg yolks into chocolate cream and then beaten egg whites. Spread evenly over second layer and freeze again.

To serve, turn cake tin onto large round plate. Gently rub a hot cloth over surface and sides of tin. The ice-cream should drop out on to the plate like a cake.

If you have difficulty, run a knife around the edge of the cake tin and then rub a hot cloth over the surface of the tin.

Note: This looks wonderful when served at a dinner party garnished with fresh flowers or maraschino stemmed cherries. It is also a nice change for Christmas dinner dessert if you tire of the traditional plum pudding. The cassata can be placed in the freezer on its serving platter ready for use.

Serves 10

Banavo Crêpe

2 avocados
2 bananas
2 tablespoons honey
juice of 1/2 lemon
1 teaspoon raw sugar
1/2 teaspoon cinnamon
4 prepared crêpes

Mash avocado and banana with honey and lemon juice. Spread over half of cooked crêpe. Fold over and quickly brown in butter on both sides until heated through.

Sprinkle with cinnamon and sugar to serve, and cream or ice-cream if desired. Slices of avocado or banana can provide an excellent finishing touch.

Serves 4-6

Avocado Yoghurt Dessert Loaf

Weight-conscious people will love this healthful, yoghurt-based, ice-cream loaf.

400 g low-fat plain
   yoghurt
2 tablespoons honey
1 large avocado
1/2 teaspoon vanilla
   essence
2 teaspoons grated
   orange rind
1 egg white

Mash avocado with a little of the yoghurt or blend in a blender until smooth. Combine the remaining yoghurt, honey, vanilla essence and orange rind with the avocado and mix well. Pour into loaf tray and freeze for about 1 hour, or until mixture is beginning to set. Beat ice-cream to mix in the ice crystals. Beat egg white until stiff and fold gently into ice-cream. Return to freezer after smoothing ice-cream evenly on top. Freeze until set.

Serves 4

Banavo crêpe

INDEX

Printed in Singapore